**Editor**

Erica N. Russikoff, M.A.

**Illustrator**

Clint McKnight

**Cover Artist**

Brenda DiAntonis

**Editor in Chief**

Ina Massler Levin, M.A.

**Creative Director**

Karen J. Goldfluss, M.S. Ed.

**Art Coordinator**

Renée Christine Yates

**Imaging**

Rosa C. See

**Publisher**

*Mary D. Smith, M.S. Ed.*

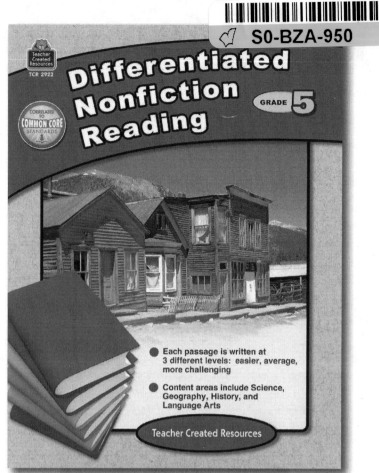

TCR 2922

**Differentiated Nonfiction Reading** GRADE 5

- Each passage is written at 3 different levels: easier, average, more challenging
- Content areas include Science, Geography, History, and Language Arts

Teacher Created Resources

**Author**

Debra J. Housel, M.S. Ed.

CORRELATED TO COMMON CORE STANDARDS

Correlations to the Common Core State Standards can be found at *http://www.teachercreated.com/standards/*.

The classroom teacher may reproduce the materials in this book and/or CD for use in a single classroom only. The reproduction of any part of this book and/or CD for other classrooms or for an entire school or school system is strictly prohibited. No part of this publication may be transmitted or recorded in any form without written permission from the publisher with the exception of electronic material, which may be stored on the purchaser's computer only.

**Teacher Created Resources, Inc.**

6421 Industry Way
Westminster, CA 92683
www.teachercreated.com

ISBN: 978-1-4206-2922-4

©2010 Teacher Created Resources, Inc.
Reprinted, 2013
Made in U.S.A.

Teacher Created Resources

# Table of Contents

# Introduction

If you are like most teachers, your classroom includes a wide variety of students: average students, English language learners, gifted students, and learning disabled students. You may be expected to get your diverse student population, including special education students and those for whom English is a second language, to master grade-level, content-area material. That's a challenging task and one that requires grade-level, content-area materials written at several levels. *Differentiated Nonfiction Reading* was written specifically to help you respond to the demands of your state and local standards while meeting the needs of your students.

## Purpose of This Book

Each passage in *Differentiated Nonfiction Reading* covers a grade-level appropriate curriculum topic in science, geography, history, or language arts. The Mid-continent Research for Education and Learning (McREL) standard and benchmark related to each passage is listed on pages 9–12.

Each content-area passage is written at three different levels: easy (below grade level), average (at grade level), and challenging (above grade level). After each passage is a set of comprehension questions that all of your students will answer. This enables your students to access the text and concepts at their instructional—rather than frustration—level, while requiring them to meet objective standards, just as they must do on standardized assessments.

## Prepare Your Students to Read Content-Area Text

You can prepare your students to read the passages in *Differentiated Nonfiction Reading* by daily reading aloud a short nonfiction selection from another source. Reading content-area text aloud is critical to developing your students' ability to read it themselves.

Discussing content-area concepts with your class is also very important. Remember, however, that discussion can never replace reading aloud since people do not speak using the vocabulary and complex sentence structures of written language.

## Readability

All of the passages in *Differentiated Nonfiction Reading* have a reading level that has been calculated by the Flesch-Kincaid Readability Formula. This formula, built into Microsoft Word®, determines a text's readability by calculating the number of words, syllables, and sentences.

Each passage is presented at three levels: easy, average, and challenging. *Easy* is below fifth-grade level; *average* is at fifth-grade level; and *challenging* is above fifth-grade level. The chart on page 13 shows you the specific reading levels of every passage.

To ensure that only you know the reading level at which each student is working, the levels are not printed on the passages. Instead, at the top of the page is a set of books with a specific pattern that will allow you to quickly match students and passages.

| Pattern | | | |
| --- | --- | --- | --- |
| **Reading Level** | **easy** (below grade level) | **average** (at grade level) | **challenging** (above grade level) |

# Introduction (cont.)

## Essential Comprehension Skills

Comprehension is the primary goal of any reading task. Students who comprehend expository text not only do better on tests, but they also have more opportunities in life. *Differentiated Nonfiction Reading* will help you to promote the foundation of comprehension skills necessary for a lifetime of learning. The questions following each passage always appear in the same order and cover six vital comprehension skills:

1. **Locating facts**—Questions based on exactly what the text states—*who, what, when, where, why,* and *how many*

2. **Understanding vocabulary in context**—Questions based on the ability to infer word meaning from the syntax and semantics of the surrounding text, as well as the ability to recognize known synonyms and antonyms for a newly encountered word

3. **Determining sequence**—Questions based on chronological order—what happened *first, last,* and *in between*

4. **Identifying conditions**—Questions that ask students to identify similarities and differences or notice cause-and-effect relationships

5. **Making inferences**—Questions that require students to evaluate, make decisions, and draw logical conclusions

6. **Analyzing and visualizing**—Questions that make students draw upon their schema and/or visualization skills to select the correct response (Visualization reinforces the important skill of picturing the text.)

## How to Use This Book

You can choose to do whole-class or independent practice. For whole-group practice, you can:

1. Distribute the passages based on students' instructional reading levels.

2. Have students read the text silently and answer the questions either on the comprehension questions page or on one of the Answer Sheets on pages 94–95.

3. Collect all of the papers and score them.

4. Return the comprehension questions pages or Answer Sheets to the students, and discuss how they determined their answers.

5. Point out how students had to use their background knowledge to answer certain questions.

You may distribute the passages without revealing the different levels. There are several ways to approach this. If you do not want your students to be aware that the passages are differentiated, organize the passages in small piles by seating arrangement. Then, when you approach a group of desks, you have just the levels you need. An alternative is to make a pile of passages from diamonds to polka dots. Put a finger between the top two levels. Then, as you approach each student, pull the passage from the top (easy), middle (average), or bottom (challenging) layer. You will need to do this quickly and without much hesitation.

# Introduction *(cont.)*

## How to Use This Book *(cont.)*

You can also announce to your class that all students will read at their own instructional levels. Do not discuss the technicalities of how the reading levels were determined. Just state that every person is reading at his or her own level and then answering the same questions. By making this statement, you can make distributing the three different levels a straightforward process.

If you find that a student is doing well, try giving him or her the next-level-up passage the next time. If he or she displays frustration, be ready to slip the student the lower-level passage.

If you prefer to have the students work independently or in centers, follow this procedure:

1. Create a folder for each student.

2. If needed, make photocopies of the Answer Sheet on page 95 for each class member, and staple the Answer Sheet to the back of each student folder.

3. Each time you want to use a passage, place the appropriate reading level of the passage and the associated comprehension questions in each student's folder.

4. Have students retrieve their folders, read the passage, and answer the questions.

5. Go over the answers with the whole class, or check the folders individually at a convenient time.

6. As an option, you may want to provide a laminated copy of the Answer Key on page 96 in the center, so students can check their own papers.

## Teaching Multiple-Choice Response

Whichever method you choose for using this book, it's a good idea to practice as a class how to read a passage and respond to the comprehension questions. In this way, you can demonstrate your own thought processes by "thinking aloud" to figure out an answer. Essentially, this means that you tell your students your thoughts as they come to you.

First, make copies of the practice comprehension questions on page 8, and distribute them to your class. Then, make and display an overhead transparency of the practice reading passage on page 7. Next, read the passage chorally. Studies have found that students of all ages enjoy choral reading, and it is especially helpful for English language learners. Choral reading lets students practice reading fluently in a safe venue because they can read in a whisper or even drop out if they feel the need.

**Discuss Question 1:** After you've read the passage aloud, ask a student to read the first question aloud. Tell the student NOT to answer the question. Instead, read all of the answer choices aloud. Emphasize that reading the choices first is always the best way to approach any multiple-choice question. Since this question is about *locating facts*, reread the first paragraph of the passage aloud as the class follows along. Have the students reread the question silently and make a selection based on the information found. Ask a student who gives the correct response (C) to explain his or her reasoning. Explain that the first question is always the easiest because the fact is stated right in the passage.

# Introduction *(cont.)*

## Teaching Multiple-Choice Response *(cont.)*

**Discuss Question 2:** The second question is about the *vocabulary* word shown in boldfaced print in the passage. Ask a student to read the question aloud. Teach your students to reread the sentence before, the sentence with, and the sentence after the vocabulary word in the passage. This will give them a context and help them to figure out what the word means. Then, have them substitute the word choices given for the vocabulary term in the passage. For each choice, they should reread the sentence with the substituted word and ask themselves, "Does this make sense?" This will help them to identify the best choice. One by one, substitute the words into the sentence, and read the sentence aloud. It will be obvious which one makes the most sense (A).

**Discuss Question 3:** The third question asks about *sequence*. Ask a student to read the question aloud. Write the choices on chart paper or the board. As a class, determine their order of occurrence, and write the numbers one through four next to them. Then, reread the question and make the correct choice (B).

**Discuss Question 4:** The fourth question is about *cause and effect* or *similarities and differences*. Ask a student to read the question aloud. Teach your students to look for the key words in the question ("pump water down") and search for those specific words in the passage. Explain that they may need to look for synonyms for the key words. For this question, ask your students to show where they found the correct response in the passage. Have students explain in their own words how they figured out the correct answer (D). This may be time-consuming at first, but it is an excellent way to help your students learn from each other.

**Discuss Question 5:** The fifth question asks students to make an *inference*. Ask a student to read the question aloud. Tell your students your thoughts as they occur to you, such as: "Well, the article didn't say that it is free to generate geothermal power, so that one's questionable. The article did say that geothermal energy comes from Earth, not from the sun, air, and water. So I'll get rid of that choice. We do have a lot of water, and in most places, that's what is forced down into Earth to make the steam. But you need to have a place where Earth is really hot near its surface, so it's not just a matter of having a water supply. I don't think that's the best choice here. Let's look back at the passage . . . it does state that there's an endless amount of heat rising from Earth, and we know that fossil fuels will soon be used up. Something that's endless cannot be used up, so I'm going to select D."

**Discuss Question 6:** The sixth question calls for *analysis* or *visualization*. With such questions, some of the answers may be stated in the passage, but others may have different wording. Sometimes one or more of the answers must be visualized to ascertain the correct response.

After having a student read the question aloud, you can say, "This one is tricky. It's asking me to choose the one that *isn't* instead of the one that *is*. First, let's look at all the choices. Then, we can ask ourselves which ones are problems with geothermal power. Only one of these is not an issue." Then, read the answer choices aloud and eliminate them one by one. Point out that the passage states that geothermal energy does not pollute groundwater, which is how you identify the correct answer (C).

## Frequent Practice Is Ideal

The passages and comprehension questions in *Differentiated Nonfiction Reading* are time-efficient, allowing your students to practice these skills often. The more your students practice reading and responding to content-area comprehension questions, the more confident and competent they will become. Set aside time to allow your class to do every passage. If you do so, you'll be pleased with your students' improved comprehension of any nonfiction text, both within your classroom and beyond its walls.

# Geothermal Power

Our Earth has a layer of hot rock below its c_____ area called the mantle. Where groundwater touches these hot rocks, it changes into stea_____am enables people to make electricity without causing pollution. It's called geothermal p_____eans Earth, and *thermal* means heat.

Italians built the first geothermal power_____. They found a place where steam rose from the ground. They trapped the steam and se_____es to turbines. Turbines are big and round and can spin very quickly. The steam made t_____n, which **generated** electrical power.

In most places, steam does not come up c_____tead, power stations pump water down to the mantle. Some of this water returns as ste_____rbines rotate and create electricity.

Geothermal energy is good for Earth an_____t does not damage the air, water, or soil. However, the steam can bring up minera_____the turbines. Also, workers must be careful around the steam, or they could get burned.

Someday all of the fossil fuels will be used up. Geothermal power can never get used up. That's why people hope to find more places and better ways to use geothermal power.

# Geothermal Power

**Directions: Darken the best answer choice.**

1. "Geothermal" means _____ from Earth.
   - Ⓐ steam
   - Ⓑ energy
   - Ⓒ heat
   - Ⓓ water

2. The word **generated** means
   - Ⓐ made.
   - Ⓑ used.
   - Ⓒ opened.
   - Ⓓ wasted.

3. Of the following choices, which occurs last?
   - Ⓐ Steam moves turbines.
   - Ⓑ Electricity goes to homes.
   - Ⓒ Steam is trapped in pipes.
   - Ⓓ Electrical power is made.

4. Why would people pump water down to a layer of hot rock?
   - Ⓐ to cool Earth's mantle
   - Ⓑ to prevent steam from escaping
   - Ⓒ to bring minerals to Earth's surface
   - Ⓓ to create steam

5. Why can't geothermal power get used up as fossil fuels can?
   - Ⓐ It costs nothing to generate geothermal power.
   - Ⓑ Scientists know how to make geothermal energy from the sun, air, and water.
   - Ⓒ We have a huge supply of water, which is what gives us geothermal power.
   - Ⓓ There's an endless supply of heat coming from within Earth.

6. Which is *not* a problem related to geothermal power?
   - Ⓐ Minerals can build up on the turbines.
   - Ⓑ There are just a few places to tap the power.
   - Ⓒ It causes salt to build up and damage the groundwater.
   - Ⓓ The steam is dangerous if it comes in contact with workers.

# Standards Correlation

Each passage and comprehension question in *Differentiated Nonfiction Reading* meets at least one of the following standards and benchmarks, which are used with permission from McREL. Copyright 2010 McREL. Mid-continent Research for Education and Learning, 4601 DTC Boulevard, Suite 500, Denver, CO 80237. Telephone: 303-337-0990. Web site: *www.mcrel.org/standards-benchmarks*. Visit *www.teachercreated.com/standards/* for correlations to the Common Core State Standards.

| Standards and Benchmarks | Passage Title | Pages |
|---|---|---|
| **SCIENCE** | | |
| **Standard 5. Understands the structure and function of cells and organisms**<br><br>**Benchmark 1.** Knows that plants and animals progress through life cycles of birth, growth and development, reproduction, and death; the details of these life cycles are different for different organisms<br><br>**Benchmark 2.** Knows that living organisms have distinct structures and body systems that serve specific functions in growth, survival, and reproduction | Gray Whales:  Giants of the Sea | 14–17 |
| **Standard 8. Understands the structure and properties of matter**<br><br>**Benchmark 1.** Knows that matter has different states (i.e., solid, liquid, gas) and that each state has distinct physical properties; some common materials, such as water, can be changed from one state to another by heating or cooling<br><br>**Benchmark 2.** Knows that the mass of a material remains constant whether it is together, in parts, or in a different state<br><br>**Benchmark 3.** Knows that substances can be classified by their physical and chemical properties (e.g., magnetism, conductivity, density, solubility, boiling and melting points) | Lead  The Original Heavy Metal | 18–21 |
| **Standard 10. Understands forces and motion**<br><br>**Benchmark 1.** Knows that magnets attract and repel each other and attract certain other materials (e.g., iron, steel)<br><br>**Benchmark 2.** Knows that Earth's gravity pulls any object toward it without touching it<br><br>**Benchmark 5.** Knows that when a force is applied to an object, the object either speeds up, slows down, or goes in a different direction<br><br>**Benchmark 6.** Knows the relationship between the strength of a force and its effect on an object (e.g., the greater the force, the greater the change in motion; the more massive the object, the smaller the effect of a given force) | Natural Forces | 22–25 |

# Standards Correlation (cont.)

| Standards and Benchmarks | Passage Title | Pages |
|---|---|---|
| **SCIENCE** *(cont.)* | | |
| **Standard 13. Understands the scientific enterprise**<br><br>**Benchmark 1.** Knows that people of all ages, backgrounds, and groups have made contributions to science and technology throughout history<br><br>**Benchmark 2.** Knows that although people using scientific inquiry have learned much about the objects, events, and phenomena in nature, science is an ongoing process and will never be finished | Frances Glessner Lee, the First Crime Scene Investigator (CSI)<br><br>Storms Lend Scientists a Helping Hand | 30–33<br><br><br>26–29 |
| **GEOGRAPHY** | | |
| **Standard 7. Knows the physical processes that shape patterns on Earth's surface**<br><br>**Benchmark 1.** Knows the physical components of Earth's atmosphere (e.g., weather and climate), lithosphere (e.g., landforms, such as mountains, hills, plateaus, plains), hydrosphere (e.g., oceans, lakes, rivers), and biosphere (e.g., vegetation and biomes) | Oceans: What's Up Down There? | 34–37 |
| **Standard 12. Understands the patterns of human settlement and their causes**<br><br>**Benchmark 4.** Knows the reasons for the growth and decline of settlements (e.g., boomtowns to ghost towns in mining areas, the rise or decline of towns linked or not linked by highways or railroads, the history of company or single-industry towns in periods of prosperity or recession) | Ghost Towns | 38–41 |
| **Standard 14. Understands how human actions modify the physical environment**<br><br>**Benchmark 1.** Knows the ways in which people alter the physical environment<br><br>**Benchmark 2.** Knows the ways in which the physical environment is stressed by human activities | Wildfire! | 42–45 |
| **Standard 15. Understands how physical systems affect human systems**<br><br>**Benchmark 4.** Knows natural hazards that occur in the physical environment (e.g., floods, windstorms, tornadoes, earthquakes) | Wildfire!<br><br>A Major Disaster: The Indian Ocean Tsunami of 2004 | 42–45<br>46–49 |

# Standards Correlation (cont.)

| Standards and Benchmarks | Passage Title | Pages |
|---|---|---|
| **GEOGRAPHY** (cont.) | | |
| **Standard 16. Understands the changes that occur in the meaning, use, distribution, and importance of resources**<br><br>**Benchmark 1.** Knows the characteristics, location, and use of renewable resources, flow resources (e.g., running water or wind), and nonrenewable resources (e.g., fossil fuels, minerals)<br><br>**Benchmark 5.** Knows advantages and disadvantages of recycling and reusing different types of materials | Turning Waste into Fuel | 50–53 |
| **WORLD HISTORY** | | |
| **Standard 9. Understands how major religions and large-scale empires arose in the Mediterranean Basin, China, and India from 500 BCE to 300 CE**<br><br>**Benchmark 5.** Understands the fundamental elements of Chinese society under the early imperial dynasties (e.g., policies and achievements of the Qin emperor Shi Huangdi, the life of Confucius, and the fundamentals of Confucianism and Daoism) | Confucius and the Role of Government | 54–57 |
| **Standard 27. Understands how European society experienced political, economic, and cultural transformations in an age of global intercommunication between 1450 and 1750**<br><br>**Benchmark 2.** Understands significant contributions of the Renaissance and Reformation to European society (e.g., major achievements in literature, music, painting, sculpture, and architecture in 16th-century Europe; the life and accomplishments of select figures from the Renaissance to the Reformation) | Martin Luther and the Protestant Reformation | 58–61 |
| **U.S. HISTORY** | | |
| **Standard 3. Understands why the Americas attracted Europeans, why they brought enslaved Africans to their colonies, and how Europeans struggled for control of North America and the Caribbean**<br><br>**Benchmark 3.** Understands peaceful and conflicting interaction between English settlers and Native Americans in the New England, Mid-Atlantic, Chesapeake, and lower South colonies (e.g., how Native American and European societies influenced one another, differing European and Native American views of the land and its use)<br><br>**Benchmark 4.** Understands the similarities and differences in backgrounds, motivations, and occupational skills between people in the English settlements and those in the French and Spanish settlements | The French and Indian War | 62–65 |

# Standards Correlation *(cont.)*

| Standards and Benchmarks | Passage Title | Pages |
|---|---|---|
| **U.S. HISTORY** *(cont.)* | | |
| **Standard 9. Understands the United States territorial expansion between 1801 and 1861, and how it affected relations with external powers and Native Americans**<br><br>**Benchmark 1.** Understands the factors that led to U.S. territorial expansion in the Western Hemisphere (e.g., Napoleon's reasons for selling the Louisiana Territory, expeditions of American explorers and mountain men) | The Lewis and Clark Expedition | 66–69 |
| **Standard 19. Understands federal Indian policy and United States foreign policy after the Civil War**<br><br>**Benchmark 3.** Understands critical features of the Spanish-American War (e.g., conditions that led to the war with Spain in 1898, character and outcome of the war, leading personalities of the Spanish-American War) | The Spanish-American War | 70–73 |
| **LANGUAGE ARTS*** | | |
| **Standard 7. Uses reading skills and strategies to understand and interpret a variety of informational texts**<br><br>**Benchmark 1.** Uses reading skills and strategies to understand a variety of informational texts (e.g., textbooks, biographical sketches, letters, diaries, directions, procedures, magazines) | Wilma Rudolph, Olympic Champion (Brief Biography) | 74–77 |
| **Benchmark 2.** Knows the defining characteristics of a variety of informational texts (e.g., textbooks, biographical sketches, letters, diaries, directions, procedures, magazines) | Real Ghost Stories: Washington Irving (Web Site) | 78–81 |
| **Benchmark 3.** Uses text organizers (e.g., headings, topic and summary sentences, graphic features, typeface, chapter titles) to determine the main ideas and to locate information in a text | Pelorus Jack: Famous Dolphin Feared Dead (Newspaper Article) | 82–85 |
| **Benchmark 6.** Uses prior knowledge and experience to understand and respond to new information | A Big Change (E-mail) | 86–89 |
| **Benchmark 7.** Understands structural patterns or organization in informational texts (chronological, logical, or sequential order; compare-and-contrast; cause-and-effect; proposition and support) | Man's Father and Son Shot on Same Date, Eighty-One Years Apart (Magazine Feature) | 90–93 |

*Each passage in this book meets the language arts standard and some or all of these benchmarks. The language arts passages are listed here because they were designed to specifically address these benchmarks.

# Reading Levels Chart

| Content Area and Title | Easy ◆ | Average ☆ | Challenging ⬤ |
|---|---|---|---|
| **SCIENCE** | | | |
| Gray Whales: Giants of the Sea | 3.6 | 5.1 | 6.4 |
| Lead: The Original Heavy Metal | 4.2 | 5.0 | 6.0 |
| Natural Forces | 4.0 | 5.4 | 6.9 |
| Storms Lend Scientists a Helping Hand | 3.7 | 5.1 | 6.5 |
| Frances Glessner Lee, the First Crime Scene Investigator (CSI) | 3.6 | 5.3 | 6.7 |
| **GEOGRAPHY** | | | |
| Oceans: What's Up Down There? | 4.2 | 5.1 | 6.6 |
| Ghost Towns | 4.0 | 5.6 | 6.7 |
| Wildfire! | 4.0 | 5.1 | 6.9 |
| A Major Disaster: The Indian Ocean Tsunami of 2004 | 4.4 | 5.4 | 6.5 |
| Turning Waste into Fuel | 4.1 | 5.0 | 6.5 |
| **WORLD AND U.S. HISTORY** | | | |
| Confucius and the Role of Government | 4.2 | 5.2 | 6.8 |
| Martin Luther and the Protestant Reformation | 4.3 | 5.4 | 6.7 |
| The French and Indian War | 4.3 | 5.2 | 6.8 |
| The Lewis and Clark Expedition | 4.5 | 5.6 | 6.7 |
| The Spanish-American War | 4.4 | 5.5 | 6.7 |
| **LANGUAGE ARTS** | | | |
| Wilma Rudolph, Olympic Champion (Brief Biography) | 4.5 | 5.4 | 6.5 |
| Real Ghost Stories: Washington Irving (Web Site) | 4.4 | 5.5 | 6.6 |
| Pelorus Jack: Famous Dolphin Feared Dead (Newspaper Article) | 4.2 | 5.3 | 6.5 |
| A Big Change (E-mail) | 4.3 | 5.4 | 6.2 |
| Man's Father and Son Shot on Same Date, Eighty-One Years Apart (Magazine Feature) | 4.2 | 5.2 | 6.3 |

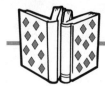

# Gray Whales: Giants of the Sea

Gray whales are huge. Adults grow up to fifty feet long. That's the length of a Greyhound bus! They can weigh twenty to forty tons. The females are larger and heavier than males. It takes a whale a long time to grow up, too. A female can first have a baby when she is eight years old. But, she may still have a long life ahead of her. These whales can reach the age of sixty.

Gray whales eat small clams, worms, and amphipods (like tiny shrimp) from the sea floor. They dive to the bottom and pick up a mouthful of mud. Then, they surface and force the mud through 140–180 filtering plates. These plates, called baleen, are made of the same material as our toenails. The baleen hang from each side of the upper jaw and trap the tiny animals. The whale licks them off with its tongue. Whales must do this again and again because they eat 7 percent of their body weight each day. If they don't, they will not stay healthy.

The gray whales spend their summer in waters off Alaska. They spend the winter near Baja, California. That's where the females give birth and raise their babies. A female has a baby every other year. She carries the calf for thirteen months. When she gives birth to the calf, it is fifteen feet long and weighs 2,000 pounds!

At birth, the gray whale calf has smooth, gray skin. By the time it is a year old, its skin is covered in barnacles and looks blotchy. The barnacles attach to the whale's body. It's the only place they can live. The barnacles eat tiny food in the water.

The whale babies nurse for seven months. They drink two gallons of milk each time. Whale milk is 52 percent fat. Cow milk is just 4 percent fat. Whale milk is so fatty because the calf must grow a layer of blubber. It needs warmth for the annual migration. Each year, these whales migrate about 12,000 miles up and down the cold waters of the Pacific coast. They swim 6,000 miles each way. They have the second-longest migration of any animal. In forty years of migrating, a gray whale swims the distance to the moon and back!

Sometimes a gray whale makes a huge leap from the water. It exposes most of its body length. But, no one knows the reason for **breeching**. Some scientists think that they are "talking" to other whales. Others say it is like our scratching. The whales are trying to remove itchy parasites from their skin. Maybe they are just having fun and enjoying being a whale!

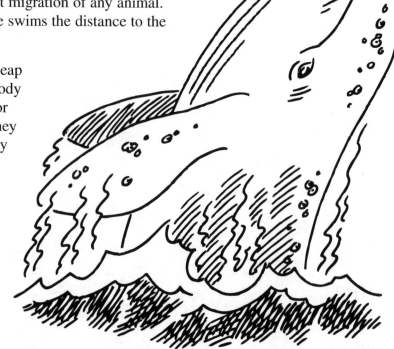

# Gray Whales: Giants of the Sea

Gray whales are huge. Adults grow up to fifty feet long, which is about the length of a Greyhound bus. The adults can weigh twenty to forty tons, with the females being larger and heavier than males. It takes a whale a long time to mature, and a female can have her first baby only when she reaches eight years old. However, at eight, she is still quite young since these whales can live for sixty years.

Gray whales are large, but their food is not. They eat small clams, worms, and amphipods (such as tiny shrimp) from the sea floor. They dive to the bottom, pick up a mouthful of mud, go up to the surface, and force the mud through 140–180 filtering plates. These plates are called baleen. They hang from each side of the upper jaw and are made of the same material as our toenails. The baleen plates trap the tiny animals. The whale licks them off with its tongue and swallows them whole. Whales repeat this process over and over. They are eating machines. They must eat 7 percent of their body weight daily in order to stay healthy.

In summer, the gray whales live in waters off Alaska. Then, they travel down the shore of North America to spend the winter near Baja California, Mexico. In this warmer water, the females give birth and raise their babies. A female has a baby every other year. She carries the calf for thirteen months. When she gives birth to the calf, it is fifteen feet long and weighs 2,000 pounds!

At birth, the gray whale calf has smooth, gray skin, but by the time it is one year old, barnacles have covered the skin so it looks blotchy. The barnacles attach to the whale's body. They eat microscopic food in the water.

The whale calves nurse for seven months, drinking two gallons of milk each time. Cow milk is just 4 percent fat, while whale milk is 52 percent fat. Whale milk is so rich because the calf must grow a layer of blubber. It needs this warmth for the annual migration. Each year, these whales migrate about 12,000 miles up and down the cold waters of the Pacific coast. They swim 6,000 miles each way. This gives them the second-longest migration of any animal. In forty years of migrating, a gray whale swims the distance to the moon and back!

Sometimes people see a gray whale make a huge leap from the water that exposes most of its body length, but no one knows the reason for **breeching**. Some scientists think that this is a way of "talking" to other whales. Other scientists say the behavior is similar to our scratching. The whales want to get itchy parasites off of their skin. Maybe they are just having fun and enjoying being whales!

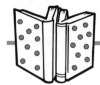

# Gray Whales: Giants of the Sea

Gray whales are huge. Adults grow up to fifty feet long, or about the length of a Greyhound bus. The adults can weigh twenty to forty tons, and the females are larger and heavier than males. It takes a whale a long time to mature; a female cannot have a baby until she is at least eight years old. At eight, she is still quite young considering that these whales can live for sixty years.

Gray whales eat small clams, worms, and amphipods (like tiny shrimp) from the sea floor. They dive to the bottom, pick up a mouthful of mud, return to the surface, and force the mud through 140–180 filtering plates. These plates, called baleen, hang from each side of the upper jaw and are made of the same material as our toenails. The baleen plates trap the tiny animals, which the whale licks off with its tongue. Whales repeat this process constantly because they must consume 7 percent of their body weight daily in order to stay healthy.

During summer, the gray whales live in waters off Alaska. Then, they travel along the shore of the North American continent to spend their winter near Baja, California. In this warmer water, the females give birth and raise their babies. A female has a baby every other year. She carries the calf for thirteen months. When she gives birth to the calf, it is fifteen feet long and weighs one ton!

At birth, the gray whale calf has smooth, gray skin, but by the time it is one year old, barnacles have covered the skin so it looks blotchy. The barnacles attach to the whale's body and eat microscopic food in the water.

The whale calves nurse for seven months, drinking two gallons of milk each time. Cow milk is just 4 percent fat, while whale milk is 52 percent fat. Whale milk is so fatty because the calf must grow a layer of blubber. It needs warmth for the annual migration. Each year, these whales migrate about 12,000 miles up and down the cold waters of the Pacific coast. They swim 6,000 miles each way, giving them the distinction of having the second-longest migration of any animal. In forty years of migrating, a gray whale swims the distance to the moon and back!

Sometimes people observe a gray whale making a huge leap from the water that exposes most of its body length. Yet nobody knows the reason for **breeching**. Some scientists think that this is a method of "talking" to other whales. Others say the behavior is similar to our scratching, and the whales are attempting to remove itchy parasites from their skin. Perhaps they are just having fun and enjoying being whales!

# Gray Whales: Giants of the Sea

**Directions: Darken the best answer choice.**

1. Gray whales eat
   - Ⓐ baleen.
   - Ⓑ amphipods.
   - Ⓒ mud.
   - Ⓓ fish.

2. The word **breeching** means
   - Ⓐ leaping.
   - Ⓑ diving.
   - Ⓒ squealing.
   - Ⓓ swimming.

3. Which event happens second in a female gray whale's life?
   - Ⓐ She has a calf.
   - Ⓑ She makes her first journey to Alaska.
   - Ⓒ She makes her first journey to Baja California.
   - Ⓓ She drinks milk from her mother.

4. In which body of water would you expect to find a gray whale?
   - Ⓐ the Atlantic Ocean
   - Ⓑ the Indian Ocean
   - Ⓒ the Southern Ocean
   - Ⓓ the Pacific Ocean

5. If a disease killed a lot of gray whales, you would expect the barnacle population to
   - Ⓐ become extinct.
   - Ⓑ increase dramatically.
   - Ⓒ decrease dramatically.
   - Ⓓ remain the same.

6. Whale milk has _____ times more fat than cow milk.
   - Ⓐ eight
   - Ⓑ ten
   - Ⓒ twelve
   - Ⓓ thirteen

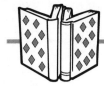

# Lead:  The Original Heavy Metal

When the "lead" point of your pencil wears down, you sharpen it.  But it is not actually lead.  It is graphite.  Lead is an element.  An element is a substance that cannot be broken down into parts.  Lead is also a heavy metal.  People have been melting lead and forming it into useful items since at least 6400 BCE.  Now, it is used in car batteries, fishing sinkers, bullets, and electronics.  It is in the red and yellow glazes used on pottery, too.

Lead does not conduct electricity well.  Nor does it let radiation through.  Have you ever had an x-ray of your teeth taken?  If so, you may recall that the x-ray operator put a big, heavy "bib" on you.  It was filled with lead.  Why?  The x-rays could not go through the bib.  It protected your body.  Lead does not corrode.  This means that it doesn't break down or rust easily.  That is why reactive chemicals are put in lead-lined containers.  One such chemical is sulfuric acid.  This acid can dissolve many things—even a lot of metals!  But not lead.

Lead's chemical symbol is "Pb."  It comes from *plumbum*, its Latin name.  The Romans used lead pipes to carry water.  The words "plumbing" and "plumber" come from a combination of these pipes and lead's Latin name.  But there's a problem with using lead pipes to carry drinking water.  Sometimes a little lead gets into the water.  Humans should not **ingest** lead.  It is toxic.  It can build up inside a person and cause lead poisoning.  Lead used to be in household paints.  Some old homes have layers of this paint.  If the paint peels and a toddler eats it, the child can get ill.  It can even hurt the child's brain.

Lead is dug or mined from the ground as ore.  This ore is a solid.  It is almost always a mixture of lead, copper, zinc, and silver.  Heating the ore separates each element from the others.  It makes the ore melt.  Lead melts at a very high temperature: 621.5°F.

James Watt, who invented the steam engine, had a dream about lead.  He dreamed that he was walking in the rain.  And the raindrops were tiny, round, lead balls!  He had the dream several times.  He thought that it meant he should combine lead and water.  He decided to melt lead in a church steeple.  Then, he threw the hot, liquid lead over the edge of the church roof.  It "rained down" into the water-filled moat around the church.  He rushed down to see what had happened.  When the lead struck the water, it instantly turned into thousands of tiny, perfect balls.  Watt had just discovered how to make buckshot (tiny, round bullets).  Buckshot is still made by dropping hot lead into water.  The mass (amount of matter) of the lead does not change.  It remains the same whether it is solid or liquid.  It stays the same if it is in a big chunk or millions of tiny, round balls.

Few people know that lead is used in televisions and computer monitors.  This makes it dangerous to throw out these items.  Putting them into the trash means that they end up in a landfill.  The lead can leak out and pollute the groundwater near the dump.  This is why TVs and computer monitors should be taken to a recycling center.  And there's another reason why this lead should be recycled.  We are running out of lead!  Some scientists think that we will run out of lead within your lifetime.  As a result, reclaiming lead from scrap (unwanted) items is becoming more common and more profitable.

# Lead: The Original Heavy Metal

When the "lead" point of your pencil wears down, you sharpen it. But it is not actually lead; it is graphite. Lead is an element. An element is a substance that cannot be broken down into parts. Lead is also a heavy metal. People have been melting lead and forming it into useful items since at least 6400 BCE. Now, it is used in car batteries, fishing sinkers, bullets, and electronics. It is also in the red and yellow glazes used on pottery.

Lead does not conduct electricity well nor does it let radiation through. Have you ever had an x-ray of your teeth taken? If so, you may recall that the x-ray operator put a big, heavy "bib" on you. It was filled with lead. Why? The x-rays could not go through the bib. It protected your body. Lead does not corrode either. This means that it doesn't break down or rust easily. That is why reactive chemicals are put in lead-lined containers. One such chemical is sulfuric acid. This acid can dissolve many things—even a lot of metals—but not lead.

Lead's chemical symbol is "Pb." It comes from *plumbum*, its Latin name. The Romans used lead pipes to carry water. The words "plumbing" and "plumber" come from a combination of these pipes and lead's Latin name. However, there's a problem with using lead pipes to carry drinking water. Sometimes a little lead gets into the water. Humans should not **ingest** lead because it is toxic. It can build up inside a person and cause lead poisoning. Before people realized this, lead was in household paints. Some old homes have layers of this paint. If the paint peels and a toddler eats it, the child can get ill. It can even hurt the child's brain.

Lead is dug or mined from the ground as ore. This ore is a solid that's almost always a mixture of lead, copper, zinc, and silver. Heating the ore makes it melt and separates each element from the others. Lead melts at a very high temperature: 621.5°F.

James Watt, who invented the steam engine, had a dream about lead. He dreamed that he was walking in the rain—and the raindrops were tiny, lead balls! He had the dream several times. He thought that it meant he should combine lead and water. He decided to melt lead in a church steeple. Then, he threw the hot, liquid lead over the edge of the church roof. It "rained down" into the water-filled moat surrounding the church. He rushed down to see what had happened. When the lead struck the water, it instantly turned into thousands of tiny, perfect balls. Watt had just discovered how to make buckshot (tiny, round bullets). Buckshot is still made by dropping hot lead into water. The mass (amount of matter) of the lead does not change. It remains the same whether it is solid or liquid. It remains the same if it is in a big chunk or millions of tiny, round balls.

Few people realize that lead is used in televisions and computer monitors. This makes it dangerous to throw out these items. Putting them into the trash means that they end up in a landfill where the lead can leak out and pollute the groundwater. This is why TVs and computer monitors should be taken to a recycling center. And there's another reason why this lead should be recycled: we are running out of lead! Some scientists estimate that we will run out of lead within your lifetime. As a result, reclaiming lead from scrap (unwanted) items is becoming more common and more profitable.

# Lead: The Original Heavy Metal

When the "lead" point of your pencil wears down, you sharpen it. But your pencil does not actually contain lead; it contains graphite. Lead is an element, which is a substance that cannot be broken down into parts. Lead is also a heavy metal. People have been melting lead and forming it into useful items since at least 6400 BCE. Today, it is used in car batteries, fishing sinkers, bullets, and electronics. It is also in the red and yellow glazes used on pottery.

Lead does not conduct electricity well nor does it let radiation pass through. If you have ever had an x-ray of your teeth taken, you may recall that the x-ray operator put a big, heavy "bib" on you. It was filled with lead to prevent the x-rays from reaching your body. The lead stopped the x-rays and protected your body. Lead does not corrode, which means that it doesn't break down or rust easily. Therefore, reactive chemicals like sulfuric acid are stored inside lead-lined containers. This acid can dissolve many things—even a lot of metals—but not lead.

Lead's chemical symbol is "Pb" from *plumbum*, its Latin name. The Romans used lead pipes to carry water. The words "plumbing" and "plumber" come from a combination of these pipes and lead's Latin name. However, there's a problem with using lead pipes to carry drinking water. Sometimes a little lead gets into the water. Humans should not **ingest** lead because it is toxic. It can build up inside a person's body and cause lead poisoning. Before people realized this, lead was in household paints. Some old homes have layers of this paint. If the paint peels and a toddler eats it, the child can get ill or even sustain brain damage.

Lead is dug or mined from the ground as ore. This ore is a solid that's almost always a mixture of lead, copper, zinc, and silver. Heating the ore makes it melt and separates each element from the others. Lead melts at a very high temperature: 621.5°F.

James Watt, who invented the steam engine, had a dream about lead. He dreamed that he was walking in the rain—and the raindrops were tiny, lead balls! He had the dream several times and thought that it meant he should combine lead and water. He melted lead in a church steeple. Then, he threw the hot, liquid lead over the edge of the church roof. It "rained down" into the water-filled moat surrounding the church. He rushed down to see what had happened. When the lead struck the water, it instantly turned into thousands of tiny, perfect balls. Watt had just discovered how to make buckshot (tiny, round bullets). Today, buckshot is still made by dropping hot lead into water. The mass (amount of matter) of the lead does not change; it remains the same whether it is solid or liquid. It remains the same if it is in a big chunk or millions of tiny, round balls.

Not many people realize that lead is used in all televisions and computer monitors, and this makes it dangerous to throw out these items. Putting them into the trash means they end up in a landfill where the lead can leak out and pollute the groundwater. All TVs and computer monitors should be taken to a recycling center. And there's another reason why this lead should be recycled: we are running out of lead! Some scientists estimate that we will run out of lead within your lifetime. As a result, reclaiming lead from scrap (unwanted) items is becoming more common and more profitable.

# Lead: The Original Heavy Metal

**Directions: Darken the best answer choice.**

1. Today, lead is used in
   - (A) pottery glazes.
   - (B) car frames.
   - (C) pipes that carry drinking water.
   - (D) pencils.

2. The word **ingest** means to
   - (A) touch.
   - (B) take in.
   - (C) throw up.
   - (D) breathe out.

3. Which event happened last?
   - (A) James Watt did a strange experiment using lead.
   - (B) Factories began making buckshot using water and liquid lead.
   - (C) Factories began making computer monitors using lead.
   - (D) James Watt dreamed about lead raindrops.

4. Lead is almost always found mixed with three other elements, but not with
   - (A) silver.
   - (B) copper.
   - (C) zinc.
   - (D) aluminum.

5. Dangerous acids are kept inside lead-lined containers because the lead is
   - (A) not going to dissolve.
   - (B) heavy.
   - (C) inexpensive.
   - (D) toxic.

6. A boy broke his arm. To take x-rays of his arm, the x-ray technician stepped behind a lead-lined wall. Why?
   - (A) The lead supports the heavy x-ray camera.
   - (B) The lead protects the technician from x-ray radiation.
   - (C) The lead is what makes the x-ray machine function.
   - (D) The lead forms the images on the x-ray film.

# Natural Forces

A force pushes or pulls to make a thing move. Our world has natural forces. Sir Isaac Newton wrote about them in his laws of motion. He said that all matter has inertia. This means that a thing stays still or moves in the same way until a force acts upon it. A book put on a desk will stay there until a force moves it. Skis will glide in a straight path down a mountain until the person wearing them does something to change direction, falls, or reaches the bottom.

Gravity is the force that pulls things on Earth toward the ground. It holds you down. Without it, you would float away. Gravity is the force that jets, helicopters, and space shuttles must **defy** to lift off our planet's surface. Large objects have powerful gravity. The sun's gravity holds all of the planets in their orbits. Earth's gravity holds our moon in orbit. The moon's gravity pulls on the world's seas as it moves around Earth. The moon's gravitational pull causes the ocean tides. In space, gravity pulls smaller objects toward larger ones. Jupiter is the biggest planet. Its gravity has pulled rocks, ice, and dust into orbit around it. It has at least sixty-three moons.

Magnetic force occurs between magnets. Magnets pull metal objects closer together or push them farther apart. Earth itself is a huge magnet. Like all magnets, it has a north pole and a south pole. A north pole and a south pole attract. Two norths or two souths will repel, or push away from each other. Magnetic levitation trains operate this way. Both the track and the base of the train are electrified as "north." This makes the surfaces repel each other. It pushes the train forward as it floats above the track. When it's time to stop, the train operator throws an electric switch. This changes the train's base to "south." Magnetic attraction causes the train to drop onto the track and stay there.

Friction is an important force. It works to slow or stop movement between surfaces that rub together. Without friction, a person who started running couldn't stop. You couldn't pick up a ball or kick it. Hikers wear boots with deep treads to increase friction. Baseball and football players wear cleats for the same reason. A soccer goalie wears gloves. This makes it easier to catch and hold the ball.

A lack of friction lets things slide. A smooth surface—such as a bowling lane—will have less friction than a rough surface like a brick. Sometimes a lack of friction is good. At other times, it's bad. Ice has little friction, which is good for skaters. They glide across it. But ice on a road is a danger. It may cause a car to slide off the road or into another car.

Drag is the force of air or water slowing down anything moving through it. Engineers design cars and planes to reduce drag. Fish have sleek bodies to move through water. To cut down on the drag in water, swimmers may shave their heads and bodies. The lack of hair makes their bodies more like those of fish. It lets them glide through the water more rapidly.

# Natural Forces

A force is anything that pushes or pulls to make an object move. Our world has natural forces that Sir Isaac Newton identified in his laws of motion. He said that all matter has inertia. Inertia means that any object stays still or moves in the same way until a force acts upon it. For example, a book placed on a desk will stay there until someone or something creates a force to move it. Inertia also means that skis will glide in a straight path down a mountain until the person wearing them does something to change direction, falls, or reaches the bottom.

Gravity is the force that pulls everything on Earth toward the ground. Gravity holds you down. Without it, you would just float away. Gravity is the force that jets, helicopters, and space shuttles must **defy** in order to escape from our planet's surface. Large objects have very strong gravity. The sun's gravity is so intense that it holds all of the planets in their orbits. Earth's gravity is so strong that it holds our moon in orbit. Our moon's gravity pulls on the world's oceans as it rotates around Earth. The moon's gravitational pull is what causes the tides in the ocean. In space, a smaller object will always fall toward a larger one. Jupiter, the largest planet, has powerful gravity. It has pulled many chunks of rock, ice, and dust into orbit around it. It has at least sixty-three moons.

Magnetic force occurs between two magnets. Magnets can pull metal objects closer together or push them farther apart. Earth itself is a huge magnet. Like all magnets, it has a north pole and a south pole. While a north pole and a south pole will attract, two norths or two souths will repel each other. Magnetic levitation trains operate on this principle. Both the track and the base of the train are electrified as "north." This makes the surfaces repel and pushes the train forward as it floats above the track. When it's time to stop the train, the operator throws an electric switch to change the train's base to "south." Magnetic attraction causes it to drop onto the track and stay there.

Friction is an important force that slows or stops movement between any two surfaces that rub together. Without friction, a person who started running couldn't stop. A person couldn't pick up a ball or kick it because it would slip away. Hikers wear boots with deep treads to increase friction. Baseball and football players wear cleats for the same reason. A soccer goalie wears gloves to make it easier to catch and hold the ball.

A lack of friction lets things slide. A smooth surface—such as a bowling lane—will have less friction than a rough surface, such as a brick. Sometimes a lack of friction is good; other times it's bad. Ice has little friction, which is good for skaters. They can glide across it. When ice is on a road, it is dangerous. It may cause a vehicle to slide off the road or into another vehicle.

Drag is the force of air or water slowing down anything moving through it. Engineers design jets and cars to reduce drag. Fish have sleek bodies to move efficiently through water. To cut down on drag, swimmers may shave their heads and bodies. The lack of hair makes their bodies more like fish, so they can glide through the water quickly.

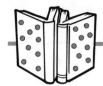

# Natural Forces

A force is anything that pushes or pulls to make an object move. Sir Isaac Newton identified natural forces in his laws of motion. He said that all matter has inertia, which means that an object stays still or moves in the same way until a force acts upon it. A book placed on a desk will stay there unless someone or something creates a force to move it. Inertia causes skis to glide in a straight path down a mountain until the person wearing them falls, does something to change direction, or reaches the bottom.

Gravity is the force that pulls everything on Earth toward the ground. Gravity holds you down and prevents you from floating away. It is the force that jets, helicopters, and space shuttles must **defy** in order to lift off our planet's surface. Large objects have very strong gravity. The sun's gravity is so strong that it holds all of the planets in their orbits. Earth's gravity holds our moon in orbit. As it rotates around Earth, our moon's gravity pulls on the water in the world's oceans and causes the tides. In space, a larger object's gravity will always draw smaller objects toward it. Jupiter, the largest planet, has such powerful gravity that it has pulled at least sixty-three moons, and a multitude of rocks, ice chunks, and dust into orbit around it.

Magnetic force occurs between two magnets by pulling metal objects closer together or pushing them farther apart. Earth itself is a huge magnet, and like all magnets, has a north pole and a south pole. While a north pole and a south pole will attract, two norths or two souths will repel. Magnetic levitation trains operate on this principle. Both the track and the base of the train are electrified as "north," causing the surfaces to repel and pushing the train forward as it floats above the track. When it's time to stop, the train operator throws an electric switch. This changes the train's base to "south," and magnetic attraction causes it to drop onto the track and stay there.

Friction is an important force that slows or stops movement between any two surfaces that rub together. Without friction, a person who started running couldn't stop, and you couldn't pick up a ball or kick it because it would slip away. Hikers wear boots with deep treads to increase friction; baseball and football players wear cleats for the same reason. A soccer goalie wears gloves to make it easier to catch and hold the ball.

A lack of friction lets things slide. A smooth surface—such as a bowling lane—will have less friction than a rough surface, such as a brick. Sometimes a lack of friction is good, and at other times it's bad. Ice has little friction, which allows skaters to glide across it. However, when ice is on a road, it is dangerous. It may cause a vehicle to slide off the road or careen into another vehicle.

Engineers design jets and cars to reduce drag, which is the force of air or water slowing down anything moving through it. Fish have sleek bodies to move efficiently through water. To reduce drag, swimmers may shave their heads and bodies. The lack of hair makes their bodies more like fish, enabling them to glide through the water rapidly.

# Natural Forces

**Directions:** Darken the best answer choice.

1. The force of gravity in space
   Ⓐ pulls a larger object toward a smaller one.
   Ⓑ pulls a smaller object toward a bigger one.
   Ⓒ causes magnetic forces.
   Ⓓ comes from inertia.

2. The word **defy** means to
   Ⓐ oppose; resist.
   Ⓑ cooperate.
   Ⓒ cling.
   Ⓓ destroy.

3. Which event happened third?
   Ⓐ The moon's gravity pulled on Earth's oceans.
   Ⓑ Earth's gravity held the moon in orbit.
   Ⓒ The oceans' tides rose and fell.
   Ⓓ The moon revolved around Earth.

4. For an in-line skater to roll across a flat surface, she must overcome the force of
   Ⓐ gravity.
   Ⓑ magnetism.
   Ⓒ friction.
   Ⓓ inertia.

5. A magnetic levitation train will move when the track is charged as
   Ⓐ "south" and the bottom of the train is charged as "north."
   Ⓑ "north" and the bottom of the train is charged as "south."
   Ⓒ "south" and the bottom of the train is charged "south."
   Ⓓ all of the above.

6. Earth's gravity is
   Ⓐ stronger than the moon's gravity.
   Ⓑ stronger than the sun's gravity.
   Ⓒ stronger than Jupiter's gravity.
   Ⓓ weaker than the moon's gravity.

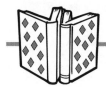

# Storms Lend Scientists a Helping Hand

Once in a while, a storm can be a scientist's best friend. The best-known example is of Ben Franklin's kite experiment. Ben discovered that lightning was electricity. He found out from a thunderstorm. In June 1752, Ben tied a key to the end of a kite string. Then, he flew the kite during a lightning storm. A lightning bolt struck his kite and moved down the line. It hit the key. Ben touched the key. He got a shock! This proved his theory that lightning was electricity. But don't ever try this yourself! Ben was lucky that he was not killed.

**Ben Franklin**

Paleontology is the study of dinosaurs. As far as we know, no dinosaur bones were ever seen before 1811. That's when a twelve-year-old girl named Mary Anning found a huge head in a sea cliff. It was near her home in England. She and her brother liked fossils. Fossils are ancient animals and plants that turned into rocks over time. The pair searched the sea cliffs. They dug out small fossils and cleaned them. Then, they put them on their porch. Collectors came and bought them. One day, Mary and Joe dug out the big head. They had never seen anything like it. Yet they could not find its body.

Then, a huge storm hit in 1812. It gave Mary the help she needed. Wind and waves knocked rocks from the cliffs. The rest of the skeleton was exposed. It was twenty feet long. It took Mary and her brother days to dig it out. Years later, scientists named it ichthyosaur. It swam in the sea millions of years ago. No more dinosaur bones were found until 1822. That's when Mary Woodhouse Mantell found some teeth. They had turned into stone. They stuck out of a rock. They were exposed after a flood swept through the area.

Another storm gave archaeology a boost. Archaeology is the study of old societies. The Makah Native Americans lived in what is now the state of Washington. For years, they had villages along the seashore. They had an oral story. It told of a terrible storm that caused a huge landslide. A whole village was buried. This happened about 300 years ago. No one knew where to look for the **entombed** village. Its name was Ozette. Some even doubted the story was true.

Then, in the winter of 1970, high tides flooded the area. The water made objects come to the surface. One hiker came across a paddle. It was sticking out of the mud. Archaeologists rushed to the scene. They made amazing finds. When the mud buried Ozette, it was awful. Many homes and dozens of people were buried alive. However, the wet, oxygen-free conditions left a lot of the things under the ten-foot-thick clay in great shape. Many things were perfectly preserved. This is not common. Often scientists figure out what a very old thing looked like from a few of its pieces or its impression left in clay. At Ozette, scientists held actual, intact items! They found harpoons, canoes, and whistles. They dug out combs, cedar ropes, and baskets. With the careful removal of earth, four homes were found. This offered a glimpse into a lost world.

# Storms Lend Scientists a Helping Hand

Sometimes a storm may be a scientist's best friend. The best-known example is Ben Franklin's discovery that lightning was electricity. He found out from a thunderstorm. In June 1752, Ben attached a key to the end of a kite string. Then, he launched the kite into the sky during a lightning storm. A lightning bolt struck his kite, moved down the line, and hit the key. Ben touched the key and got a shock! This proved his theory that lightning was electricity. But don't ever try this yourself! It's lucky that Ben was not killed by his experiment.

**Ben Franklin**

Paleontology is the study of dinosaurs. As far as we know, no dinosaur bones were discovered prior to 1811. That's when a twelve-year-old girl named Mary Anning discovered a huge head in a sea cliff near her home in England. She and her brother were interested in fossils. Fossils are ancient animals and plants that turned into rocks over time. The pair searched the sea cliffs. They dug out small fossils, cleaned them, and sold them on their porch. Collectors bought them. One day, she and Joe dug out the big head. They had never seen anything like it. Yet they could not find its body.

Then, a huge storm hit in 1812. It provided the help that Mary needed. Wind and waves knocked rocks from the cliffs and exposed the rest of the skeleton. It was twenty feet long. It took days for Mary and her brother to dig it out. Years later, scientists named it ichthyosaur. It swam in the sea millions of years ago. No more dinosaur bones were found until 1822. That's when Mary Woodhouse Mantell saw fossilized teeth sticking out of a rock. They were exposed after a flood swept through the area.

Another storm gave archaeology a helping hand. Archaeology is the study of old societies. The Makah Native Americans lived in what is now the state of Washington. For hundreds of years, they had villages along the seashore. They had an oral story of a terrible storm that caused a huge landslide and buried a whole village. This happened about 300 years ago. No one knew where to look for the **entombed** village of Ozette. Some even doubted the story was true.

Then, in the winter of 1970, high tides flooded the village. The water made some objects surface. One hiker came across a paddle sticking out of the mud. Archaeologists rushed to the scene. They made amazing finds. When the mud buried Ozette, it was tragic. Many homes and dozens of people were buried alive. However, the wet, oxygen-free environment left a lot of the objects beneath the ten-foot-thick clay in near-perfect condition. This is very unusual. Often scientists can only figure out what a very old thing looked like from a few of its pieces or its impression left in clay. At Ozette, scientists held actual, intact items such as harpoons, canoes, whistles, combs, cedar ropes, and baskets. With the careful removal of earth, four homes emerged. This offered a thrilling glimpse into a lost world.

# Storms Lend Scientists a Helping Hand

Occasionally, a storm can be a scientist's best friend. The best-known example is Ben Franklin's discovery that lightning was electricity during a thunderstorm. In June 1752, Ben attached a key to the

**Ben Franklin**

end of a kite string and launched the kite into the sky during a lightning storm. A lightning bolt struck his kite, moved down the line, and hit the key. Ben touched the key and got a shock! Although this proved his theory that lightning was electricity, don't ever try this yourself! It's lucky that Ben wasn't killed by his experiment.

Paleontology is the study of dinosaurs. As far as we know, no dinosaur bones were discovered prior to 1811. In that year, a twelve-year-old girl named Mary Anning discovered a huge head in a sea cliff near her home in England. She and her brother were interested in fossils, which are ancient animals and plants that turned into rocks over time. The pair searched the sea cliffs, dug out small fossils, cleaned them, and sold them on their porch. Collectors came from all over to purchase them. One day, she and Joe dug out the big head. They had never seen anything like it. Even though they made a thorough search, they could not find its body.

Then, a huge storm in 1812 provided the help that Mary needed. Wind and waves knocked rocks from the cliffs, exposing the rest of the skeleton. It was twenty feet long. It took days for Mary and her brother to dig it out. Years later, scientists named it ichthyosaur and knew that it swam in the sea millions of years ago. No more dinosaur bones were found until 1822. That's when Mary Woodhouse Mantell discovered some fossilized teeth sticking out of a rock. They were exposed after a flood swept through the area.

Another storm gave archaeology a helping hand. Archaeology is the study of old civilizations. The Makah Native Americans lived in what is now the state of Washington. For centuries, they had villages along the seashore. They had an oral story of a horrific storm that caused a huge landslide and buried a whole village about 300 years ago. No one knew where to look for the **entombed** village of Ozette, and some even doubted the story was true.

Then, in the winter of 1970, high tides flooded the compound. The water made some objects surface. One hiker came across a paddle sticking out of the mud. Archaeologists who rushed to the scene made amazing finds. When the mud buried Ozette, it was tragic. Many homes and dozens of people were buried alive. However, the wet, oxygen-free environment left many objects underneath the ten-foot-thick clay perfectly preserved. This is very unusual. Often scientists can only figure out what an ancient object looked like from a few of its pieces or its impression left in clay. At Ozette, scientists held actual, intact harpoons, canoes, whistles, combs, cedar ropes, and baskets. With the careful removal of more earth, four homes emerged. This offered a thrilling glimpse into a lost world.

# Storms Lend Scientists a Helping Hand

**Directions: Darken the best answer choice.**

1. In the winter of 1970, what old Native American object did a Washington hiker find in the mud?
   - Ⓐ a basket and cedar rope
   - Ⓑ a canoe
   - Ⓒ a home
   - Ⓓ a paddle

2. The word **entombed** means
   - Ⓐ mysterious.
   - Ⓑ ancient.
   - Ⓒ buried.
   - Ⓓ missing.

3. Which event happened first?
   - Ⓐ Benjamin Franklin found out that lightning was electricity.
   - Ⓑ The village of Ozette was ruined.
   - Ⓒ Mary Woodhouse Mantell found fossilized dinosaur teeth.
   - Ⓓ Mary Anning found the first dinosaur skeleton.

4. What kind of natural disaster destroyed the village of Ozette?
   - Ⓐ a landslide
   - Ⓑ an earthquake
   - Ⓒ a wildfire
   - Ⓓ a flood

5. An archaeologist would be most excited about the discovery of
   - Ⓐ fossils of six-million-year-old plants.
   - Ⓑ new knowledge about lightning storms.
   - Ⓒ perfectly preserved saber-toothed tiger bones.
   - Ⓓ prehistoric pottery.

6. Both floods and waves crashing on a shore cause
   - Ⓐ water levels to permanently change.
   - Ⓑ erosion of soil and rock.
   - Ⓒ volcanoes to erupt.
   - Ⓓ earthquake fault lines.

# Frances Glessner Lee, The First Crime Scene Investigator (CSI)

Millions watch the *CSI* shows each week. They are some of the most popular television series of all time. Finding clues to figure out who did a murder is called forensic science. It is one of the hottest college degrees today. Each year, thousands of students take classes. They want to learn how to analyze a crime scene.

The very first crime scene investigator, or CSI, was a grandma. Her name was Frances Glessner Lee. She started Harvard's department of legal medicine. In 1936, she paid the first full-time teacher's salary. It was the nation's first program for forensic science.

In 1878, Lee was born. Her family was rich. When she grew up, she asked to go to college. At that time, most women did not go to college. Her family said no. At last, in 1930, she went to school. She was fifty-two.

Lee hated that some murders did not get solved. She believed that there was a way to solve them. As a child, she had read and reread the Sherlock Holmes' stories. She admired Holmes' keen observational skills. Lee wanted the police to use such skills to solve real crimes. She thought that the best way to do this was to recreate crime scenes in miniature. Then, they could be studied.

Lee studied real crime scenes. She became an expert. Soon, police departments around the nation asked for her help. They wanted her to train their detectives. So she made tiny crime scenes. She called them Nutshell Studies dioramas. She used them to teach officers to find clues. Some were based on real crime scenes. Most were a combination of crime scenes. Lee read about crime all of the time. She found it easy to reinvent crimes.

**Frances Glessner Lee**

It took Lee months to make each diorama. She made about three each year. She bought tiny furniture. It came from around the globe. She made many of the things and each doll herself. She had a carpenter who made exact pieces of furniture. He made the rooms or buildings, too. He lived in a house on Lee's estate. Lee spent a lot on each diorama: each one cost what a home did at that time! Each one had clues. They pointed to what had occurred.

As an **heiress**, Lee had a lot of money. She held free classes for the police. First, a diorama was put in a room. Next, the police had a limited amount of time to take notes about what they saw in it. Then, they discussed it with each other and Lee. It was not as important to solve the case as it was to find clues that might be related to the crime.

The New Hampshire State Police said that Lee helped them to understand crime. They made her an honorary captain. It's hard to assess the depth of Lee's contribution to forensic science. The ripples keep going now. Today, the Maryland Medical Examiner's Office owns all eighteen of her Nutshell Studies dioramas. They are still used in crime scene evaluation classes.

# Frances Glessner Lee, The First Crime Scene Investigator (CSI)

The *CSI* shows are some of the most popular television series ever. Finding the clues to figure out who committed a murder is called forensic science. In part due to *CSI*'s popularity, forensic science is one of the hottest college degrees today. Each year, thousands of students enroll in classes. They want to learn how to analyze a crime scene.

Few people know that the very first crime scene investigator, or CSI, was a grandma. Her name was Frances Glessner Lee. She started Harvard's department of legal medicine in 1936. She paid the first full-time professor's salary. It was the nation's first program for forensic science.

In 1878, Lee was born into a rich family. When she grew up, she asked to go to college. But at that time, most women did not earn college degrees. Her family said she could not go. Finally, in 1930, she defied them and went to school. She was fifty-two.

Lee hated that some murders went unsolved. She thought that there was a scientific way to solve them. From the time she was a child, she had read and reread the Sherlock Holmes' stories. She wanted to teach the police to use Holmes' keen observational skills to solve real crimes. She decided that the best way to do this was to recreate crime scenes in miniature. Then, they could be studied in detail.

Lee studied real crime scenes. She became an expert. Soon, police departments around the nation asked her to train their detectives. So she made miniature crime scenes. She called them Nutshell Studies dioramas. Then, she used them to teach officers to find evidence. Some of them were based on real crime scenes. Most were a combination of crime scenes. Lee read about crime all of the time. She found it easy to reinvent realistic crimes.

**Frances Glessner Lee**

It took Lee months to make each diorama. She finished about three each year. She bought miniature furniture from around the globe. She made many of the items and every doll herself. She had a carpenter who made exact pieces of furniture and the rooms or buildings. He lived in a house on Lee's estate. Lee spared no expense: each diorama cost what a home did at that time. Each one had subtle clues that pointed to what had occurred.

As an **heiress**, Lee did not need money. She held seminars for the police for free. First, a diorama was placed in a room. Next, the police had a limited amount of time to take notes about what they observed in it. Then, they came back to discuss it with each other and Lee. More important than solving the case was learning to recognize evidence that might be important to the crime.

The New Hampshire State Police felt that Lee advanced their ability to understand crime so much that they made her an honorary captain. It's hard to assess the depth of Lee's contribution to forensic science. The ripples continue today. Today, the Maryland Medical Examiner's Office owns all eighteen of her Nutshell Studies dioramas. Even now they are used in crime scene evaluation classes.

# Frances Glessner Lee,
# The First Crime Scene Investigator (CSI)

The *CSI* shows are some of the most popular television series ever. Following the clues to determine who committed a murder is called forensic science. Forensic science is one of the hottest college degrees today. Each year, thousands of students enroll in classes to learn how to evaluate a crime scene.

Few people know that the very first crime scene investigator, or CSI, was a grandmother named Frances Glessner Lee. She started Harvard's department of legal medicine in 1936 by paying the first full-time professor's salary. It was the nation's first program for forensic science.

In 1878, Lee was born into a wealthy family. When she grew up, she wanted to attend college. However, back then, it wasn't "ladylike" to earn a college degree. Her family refused to let her go. Finally, in 1930, she defied them and went to school when she was fifty-two.

Lee hated that some murders went unsolved. She was convinced that there was a scientific way to solve them. From the time she was a child, she had read and reread the Sherlock Holmes' stories. She wanted to create a way for the police to use Holmes' keen observational skills to solve actual crimes. She decided that the best way to do this was to recreate crime scenes in miniature so that they could be studied in detail.

Lee studied real crime scenes until she became an expert. Soon, law enforcement officials requested that she train their detectives. So Lee made miniature crime scenes that she called Nutshell Studies dioramas. She used them to teach officers to identify evidence. Some of them were based on real crime scenes. Most were a combination of crime scenes. Lee read about crime all of the time, so she could easily reinvent grisly crimes.

**Frances Glessner Lee**

Lee spent months making each diorama, completing about three each year. She bought miniature furniture from all over the world. She made many of the items and every doll victim. She hired a carpenter who made exact pieces of furniture and the rooms or buildings. He lived in a house on her estate. Lee spared no expense: each diorama cost what a home did at that time! Each one had subtle clues that pointed to what had occurred.

As an **heiress**, Lee needed no money. She held seminars for the police for free. A diorama was placed in a room, and the police officers had a limited amount of time to take notes about what they observed. Then, they discussed the clues with each other and Lee. More important than solving the case was learning to recognize evidence that might be related to the crime.

The New Hampshire State Police felt that Lee so advanced their ability to understand crime that they made her an honorary captain. It's hard to assess the depth of Lee's contribution to forensic science. The ripples continue today. Today, all eighteen of her Nutshell Studies dioramas are housed in the Maryland Medical Examiner's Office. They are still used in crime scene evaluation classes.

# Frances Glessner Lee, The First Crime Scene Investigator (CSI)

**Directions: Darken the best answer choice.**

1. The Nutshell Studies dioramas are currently kept
   (A) at Harvard University.
   (B) at the New Hampshire State Police department.
   (C) at the Maryland Medical Examiner's Office.
   (D) in the Frances Glessner Lee Museum.

2. An **heiress** is a
   (A) charity that gets money and/or property from a will.
   (B) child who gets money and/or property from a will.
   (C) man who gets money and/or property from a will.
   (D) woman who gets money and/or property from a will.

3. Which event happened first?
   (A) Lee funded the nation's first college forensic science department.
   (B) Lee earned a college degree.
   (C) Lee created eighteen Nutshell Studies dioramas.
   (D) Lee got married and had children.

4. Each of Lee's Nutshell Studies dioramas was
   (A) expensive to make.
   (B) based on a single, real crime scene.
   (C) based on a Sherlock Holmes' story.
   (D) eventually destroyed in a fire.

5. You can conclude that Lee was not interested in
   (A) learning about crimes.
   (B) earning money.
   (C) reading Sherlock Holmes stories.
   (D) teaching detectives how to identify clues at a crime scene.

6. Frances Glessner Lee died in 1962. If she were alive today, she would be most surprised by how
   (A) many women work in crime scene investigation.
   (B) little it costs to go to college.
   (C) many murders are solved.
   (D) few men go to college.

# Oceans: What's Up Down There?

You know that Earth has five huge bodies of water. They are the oceans. The Pacific is the deepest. It is the largest. The Atlantic is the second largest. Then, there's the Indian Ocean. The Southern Ocean surrounds Antarctica. The smallest ocean is the Arctic. The Southern and Arctic Oceans have a lot of ice. Large floating ice chunks called icebergs **originate** in these two oceans. They float into the northern Atlantic. They float into the southern Pacific. Ships must get out of their way. Hitting an iceberg could easily sink a ship.

The oceans have a lot of streams of moving water called currents. This water circulation is important. It moves heat around the world. Heated water flows from the equator toward the poles. The warm water moves in surface currents. Cold water flows from the poles. It moves toward the equator. The cool water flows in deep, underwater currents.

Far below the ocean's waves lie flat plains. There are mountains and deep trenches, too. We know this because submarines and remotely operated vehicles have gone down there. They've brought back photos. People found the continental shelves first. The continental shelves are huge plates of Earth. Each one holds both land and sea. All the land on one plate is part of the same continent. That's why Greenland is part of the North American continent. It's why Australia is its own continent. The water on a continental shelf is considered shallow. Yet it may be 490 feet deep!

The continental slopes are the edges of these shelves. Some slopes have steep sides. At the base of the slopes are the abyssal plains. These flatlands make up most of the seafloor. They are the flattest parts of Earth's crust. In some places, the plains are broken by underwater mountains. The mountains come in chains, or ridges. The largest is the Mid-Atlantic Ridge. It extends 34,000 miles. It wanders through the Atlantic, Indian, south Pacific, and Arctic Oceans.

Most often, the underwater mountains formed from lava. It came from deep-sea vents. A seamount is one of these mountains. It rises at least 3,300 feet above the seafloor. Each moment of each day, volcanoes erupt somewhere on the seafloor. Lava is always flowing. When a seamount gets tall enough, it bursts through the sea's waves. It becomes new land. This is how volcanic islands form. The Hawaiian island chain is volcanic.

The undersea world does not only have mountains. It also has deep trenches. They are like huge cracks in the ocean floor. The Mariana Trench is in the Pacific Ocean. It is more than 35,700 feet (7 miles) deep. And that's starting at the ocean floor, not its surface! It is the world's deepest sea trench. It is about seven times deeper than the Grand Canyon, too. In 1995, Japan sent a remote-controlled sub to this trench. The sub went down to the base. It sent back photos. It was the first time humans had ever seen such a sight. There is very high water pressure that far down. It wouldn't be safe for humans to go there.

# Oceans: What's Up Down There?

You know that Earth has five oceans. The Pacific is the deepest and the largest. The Atlantic is the second largest. Then, there's the Indian Ocean. The Southern Ocean surrounds Antarctica. The smallest ocean is the Arctic. The Southern and Arctic Oceans have a lot of ice. Large floating chunks of ice called icebergs **originate** in these two oceans. They float into the northern Atlantic and southern Pacific. Ships must do all they can to avoid them. Hitting an iceberg could easily sink a ship.

The oceans have many different streams of moving water called currents. This water circulation is essential. It disperses heat around the world. Heated water flows from the equator toward the poles. The warm water moves in surface currents. Cold water flows toward the equator. The cool water moves in deeper, underwater currents.

Below the ocean's waves there are flat plains. There are mountains and deep trenches, too. We know all of this because submarines and remotely operated vehicles have gone down there. They've brought back photos. People discovered the continental shelves first. The continental shelves are huge plates of Earth. Each one holds both land and sea. All the land on one plate belongs to the same continent. That's why Greenland is part of the North American continent. It's why Australia is its own continent. The water on a continental shelf is considered shallow. Yet it may be 490 feet deep!

The continental slopes are the edges of these shelves. Some slopes have steep sides. At the base of the slopes are the abyssal plains. These flatlands make up most of the seafloor. They are the flattest parts of Earth's crust. In some places, the plains are broken by tall underwater mountains. The mountains come in chains, or ridges. The largest is the Mid-Atlantic Ridge. It extends 34,000 miles as it wanders through the Atlantic, Indian, south Pacific, and Arctic Oceans.

Most often, the underwater mountains formed from lava spewing from deep-sea vents. A seamount is one of these mountains. It rises at least 3,300 feet above the seafloor. Each moment of each day, volcanoes are erupting somewhere on the ocean floor. Lava is always flowing. When a seamount gets tall enough, it bursts through the ocean's surface. Then, it is considered land. This is how all volcanic islands form, including the Hawaiian islands.

One of the most amazing parts of the undersea world is its deep trenches. They are like huge cracks in the ocean floor. The Mariana Trench is in the Pacific Ocean. It is more than 35,700 feet (7 miles) deep. And that's starting at the ocean floor, not the surface! It is the world's deepest sea trench. It is about seven times deeper than the Grand Canyon, too. In 1995, Japan sent a remote-controlled submarine to this trench. It went down to the bottom and sent back photos. It was the first time humans had ever seen such a sight. Since there is very high water pressure that far down, it wouldn't be safe for humans to go there.

# Oceans: What's Up Down There?

You have learned that Earth has five oceans. The Pacific is the deepest and the largest, and the Atlantic is the second largest. Then, there's the Indian Ocean and the Southern Ocean, which surrounds Antarctica. The smallest ocean is the Arctic. The Southern and Arctic Oceans spend a lot of the year under ice. Massive floating chunks of ice called icebergs **originate** in these two oceans. They float into the northern Atlantic and southern Pacific. Ships must avoid them. Running into an iceberg could sink a ship.

There are streams of moving water called currents in the oceans. This water circulation is essential in moving heat around the world. Heated water flows from the equator toward the poles in the surface currents. Cold water flows toward the equator in deep, underwater currents.

Beneath the ocean's waves there are mountains, deep trenches, and flat plains. We know about them because submarines and remotely operated vehicles have gone down there and photographed them. People discovered the continental shelves first. The continental shelves are huge plates of Earth. They hold both land and sea. All the land on one plate belongs to the same continent. That's why Greenland is part of the North American continent while Australia is its own continent. The water on a continental shelf is considered shallow, even though it may be 490 feet deep!

The continental slopes are the edges of these shelves. The slopes may have steep sides. At the base of the slopes are the abyssal plains. These flatlands make up most of the seafloor. Formed by fine sediment deposits, they are the flattest parts of Earth's crust. In some places, the plains are broken by tall underwater mountain chains, or ridges. The largest is the Mid-Atlantic Ridge, which extends 34,000 miles as it wanders through the Atlantic, Indian, south Pacific, and Arctic Oceans.

Usually, the underwater mountains formed from lava spewing from deep-sea vents. A seamount is one of these mountains that rises at least 3,300 feet above the seafloor. Every moment of every day, volcanoes are erupting somewhere on the ocean floor. When a seamount gets tall enough, it bursts through the ocean's surface and is considered land. This is how all volcanic islands form, including the Hawaiian island chain.

One of the most amazing parts of the undersea world is its deep trenches. They are like gigantic cracks in the ocean floor. The Mariana Trench in the Pacific Ocean is more than 35,700 feet (7 miles) deep— and that's starting at the ocean floor, not the surface! Not only is it the world's deepest sea trench, but it is seven times deeper than the Grand Canyon. In 1995, Japan sent a remote-controlled submarine to the base of this trench. It sent back the first photos people had ever seen. There is dangerously high water pressure that far down. It wouldn't be safe for humans to try to go there.

# Oceans: What's Up Down There?

**Directions: Darken the best answer choice.**

1. In the oceans, cold water always flows
   (A) along the equator.
   (B) toward the equator.
   (C) away from the equator.
   (D) on surface currents above warmer water.

2. The word **originate** means to
   (A) sink.
   (B) float.
   (C) melt.
   (D) start.

3. What natural underwater feature of Earth was discovered third?
   (A) continental shelves
   (B) icebergs
   (C) abyssal plains
   (D) the base of the Mariana Trench

4. New Zealand is considered a part of the continent of Australia. Why?
   (A) There is no underwater trench between the two land masses.
   (B) There is no seamount to separate the two land masses.
   (C) They share the same plate on Earth's crust.
   (D) Their continental slopes are similar.

5. Where is there very high water pressure?
   (A) the base of an iceberg
   (B) the base of the Mariana Trench
   (C) the base of a continental shelf
   (D) the base of the Grand Canyon

6. Seamounts formed one entire state of the United States. It is the state of
   (A) Alaska.
   (B) Hawaii.
   (C) California.
   (D) Florida.

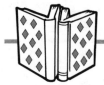

# Ghost Towns

It's a ghost town. But it's not haunted. And it's not where you go to get scared on Halloween. Just what is a ghost town? It's a place where people once lived and worked. Now, no one lives there. The place is abandoned. All that's left are buildings and the echoes of a time long ago. That's when the streets bustled with people.

Most ghost towns began as boomtowns. In a boomtown, a whole town was built quickly. This happened in some places where gold or silver was found. Many people rushed there to try to get rich. This happened several times in U.S. history. The first was the California Gold Rush. There were gold rushes in Colorado, South Dakota, and Alaska, too. All of the miners needed food, places to live, and services. Some people went to the town to open boardinghouses and general stores. They set up laundries and tailor shops. Often, the service providers were the people who made the most money. Why? The miners needed to eat and have places to sleep. This was true whether they found any gold or not.

With so many people looking for them, all of the natural resources were found fast. The gold (or silver, gemstones, or oil) ran out. People saw that there was no more money to be made. The mine was the only reason for the town. When the miners left, there was no need for lodging or other services. So the owners of those places left, too.

The ghost towns of the 19th century American West are the most common examples. You may have seen pictures of them. The photos show old wooden buildings with tumbleweeds blowing down the main street. However, a similar **phenomenon** has happened in more recent times. It happened when a whole city relied upon one industry. The fate of that industry was the fate of the city. For instance, some U.S. cities relied on the steel industry. The people who lived there worked in the steel factories. They went to the grocery stores, restaurants, and movie theaters. This meant that everyone who worked in those places relied on the steelworkers. It was like a big web. Steel was at the center. Since there is an endless need for steel, the future seemed bright. But by the late 1970s, foreign steel was cheap. It cost less than the steel made in the United States. The steel plants closed. Job after job disappeared. Many people left to get jobs in other places.

Now, most of these cities have since attracted new factories or service jobs. Although many people left the area during the crisis, some have returned. In some cases, it took decades for the region to recover.

What's the lesson to learn from ghost towns? A town or city must have more than one industry. Any place that depends upon one industry will have its fortunes rise and fall with that industry. No industry is totally safe. But if several industries support an area, its economy is stronger. It is less apt to fall apart if one of the industries fails.

# Ghost Towns

It's not haunted by ghosts. And it's not a place where you go to get scared on Halloween. Just what is a ghost town? It's a place where people once lived and worked but have since abandoned. All that remains are buildings and the memories of a time when the streets bustled with people.

Most ghost towns started out as boomtowns. In a boomtown, a whole town was built quickly. For example, in a place where gold or silver is discovered, many people rushed there to try to get rich. This happened several times during U.S. history. The first was the California Gold Rush. There were other gold rushes to Colorado, South Dakota, and Alaska. All of the miners needed food, places to live, and other services. Some people who went to the town opened boardinghouses, restaurants, general stores, laundries, and tailor shops. The service providers were usually the people who made the most money. Why? The miners needed to eat and have places to sleep whether they found any gold or not.

With so many people searching for them, all of the natural resources were quickly found. The gold (or

silver, gemstones, or oil) ran out. People realized that there was no more money to be made. The only reason for the town was for the miners, so when they left, there was no need for lodging, food, or other services. The owners of those places had to leave, too.

The ghost towns of the 19th century American West are the most dramatic examples. They lost their whole populations. You've seen pictures of them: a bunch of old wooden buildings with tumbleweeds blowing down the empty main street. However, a similar **phenomenon** has happened in more recent times as well. When an entire city relied upon one industry, the fate of that industry was the fate of the city. For instance, some U.S. cities relied on the steel industry. The people who lived there worked in the steel factories. They supported the grocery stores, restaurants, and movie theaters. Every person who worked in those places was relying on the steelworkers. It was like a big web, and at the center was steel. Since there is an endless need for steel, the future seemed bright. But by the late 1970s, foreign steel was cheaper than the steel made in the United States. The steel plants closed. Like a bunch of falling dominoes, job after job disappeared. Many people left to get jobs in other places.

Fortunately, most of these cities have since attracted new factories or service jobs. Although many people left the area during the crisis, some have returned. In some cases, it took decades for the region to recover.

What's the lesson to be learned from ghost towns? A town or city must have a variety of industries. Any place that relies solely on one industry will have its fortunes rise and fall with that industry. No industry is completely safe. But if several industries support an area, its economy is stronger. It will not collapse if one of the industries fails.

# Ghost Towns

It's not haunted by ghosts, and it's not a place where you go to get scared on Halloween. Just what is a ghost town? It's a place where many people once lived and worked but have since abandoned. All that remains are buildings and the memories of a long-ago time when the streets bustled with people.

Most ghost towns were originally boomtowns—towns that sprang up quickly, sometimes within a matter of weeks. This happened in the American West during the 19th century. Wherever gold or silver was discovered, many people rushed there, hoping to become wealthy by mining the precious metal. This happened several times during U.S. history. The first was the California Gold Rush; there were later gold rushes to Colorado, South Dakota, and Alaska. All of the miners needed food, places to live, and services, such as medical care. Some people who went to the town ran boardinghouses, restaurants, general stores, laundries, and tailor shops. These service providers were usually the people who made the most money because the miners needed to eat and have a place to sleep whether they found any gold or not.

With so many people searching, all of the natural resources were found quickly. Then, the gold (or silver, gemstones, or oil) ran out. The people realized that there was no more money to be made. The only reason for the town was for the miners, so when they left, there was no need for lodging, food, or other services. The owners of those places had to leave, too.

Since they lost their entire populations, the ghost towns of the American West are the most dramatic examples. You've seen pictures of them—a bunch of old wooden buildings with tumbleweeds blowing down the empty main street. However, a similar **phenomenon** occurred in more recent times. When an entire city relied upon one industry, the fate of the city mirrored the fate of that industry. For instance, some U.S. cities relied on the steel industry. The people who lived there worked in the steel factories. They spent their wages at the grocery stores, restaurants, and movie theaters. Each person who worked in those places was relying on the steelworkers. It was like a big web with steel at the center. Since there is a constant need for steel, the future seemed bright. But by the late 1970s, foreign steel was cheaper than the steel made in the United States, and the steel plants closed. Like falling dominoes, job after job disappeared. Many people had to leave. They sought employment in other places.

Fortunately, most of these cities have since attracted new factories or service jobs. Although many people left the area during the crisis, some have returned. In some cases, it took decades for the region to recover.

What's the lesson to be learned from ghost towns? A town or city must have a variety of industries. Any place that relies solely on one industry will have its fortunes rise and fall with that industry. No industry is completely safe. But when multiple industries support an area, its economy is less likely to collapse if one of them fails.

# Ghost Towns

**Directions:  Darken the best answer choice.**

1. Most ghost towns
   - (A) had their population abruptly disappear, and no one knows why.
   - (B) are haunted by spirits.
   - (C) had a population that grew slowly.
   - (D) were originally boomtowns.

2. The word **phenomenon** means
   - (A) tragedy.
   - (B) disappointment.
   - (C) event.
   - (D) crisis.

3. Which event occurred third?
   - (A) Silver was discovered in Colorado.
   - (B) The amount of silver was not enough to support the town.
   - (C) Miners rushed to Colorado to get the silver.
   - (D) People built a mining town in Colorado with stores, restaurants, and hotels.

4. The person most likely to get rich in a mining boomtown
   - (A) owned the general store.
   - (B) worked as a farmer.
   - (C) worked as a miner.
   - (D) provided entertainment.

5. Eastman Kodak made film and was the major employer in Rochester, New York.  When digital photography decreased film sales, Kodak laid off two-thirds of its work force, but Rochester did not become a ghost town.  Why?
   - (A) Taxes went down.
   - (B) The local economy had other industries.
   - (C) Gold was discovered and caused another boom.
   - (D) Everyone left the area to seek employment elsewhere.

6. Which natural resource is not mined?
   - (A) lumber
   - (B) diamonds
   - (C) platinum
   - (D) coal

# Wildfire!

Humans have always had an uneasy relationship with fire. Fire can be our friend or foe. As a friend, fire offers warmth, light, and heat for cooking. As a foe, an out-of-control fire can cause ruin and death.

You may have seen Smokey the Bear on a sign. He wears a hat. He holds a shovel. His sign states, "Only YOU can prevent wildfires." Perhaps you've seen ads in which Smokey tells you not to burn trash and to put out your campfire. Smokey was a real bear cub. He was rescued from a wildfire. It happened in New Mexico. He has been the symbol of fire prevention for more than sixty-five years.

Wildfires are bad for humans and wild animals. Each year, such fires ruin millions of acres. They cost billions of dollars in property loss. Such blazes often occur in places that are hot and dry. California, Texas, and Colorado are often hit. In years with little rainfall, dry tinder is everywhere. Nine out of ten wildfires are started by a person. It is not often set on purpose. A dropped cigarette, burning trash, or a child playing with matches can start a big disaster.

Lightning strikes have been starting wildfires since Earth began. Left to burn, such a fire will clear out a stand of trees every eight to fifteen years. It is part of a natural cycle. Fires allow forests to change. They free up the nutrients trapped in old, dead wood. And many old-growth trees can survive a fire because their bark can regrow.

But then people created state and national parks. They built homes near forests. When lightning started a blaze, people didn't let it burn. They put it out. They did not want to lose parklands, homes, or businesses to flames. For years, fires started by lightning were **suppressed**.

Then, in 1988, a huge fire consumed part of Yellowstone National Park. People saw that fire suppression had backfired. Why? Fire suppression had let fuel build up for years. There were a lot of leaves, branches, and dead trees lying in the forests. Also, when fire does not clear an area, too many

trees grow. They get crowded. They grow weak. There is a limited supply of water, nutrients, and light. At last they become vulnerable. Insects and diseases kill them. Scientists realized that they had to find ways to let fires clear wooded areas without hurting people, property, or wild animals. The National Parks Department changed its fire-suppression policy.

Now, lightning-strike fires are left to burn if they do not affect people's safety. Fire teams start controlled burns. This means setting a fire in a fire-dependent ecosystem. Such blazes safely reduce the amount of fuel for wildfires. The teams must be careful not to let the fire get out of hand. They must consider weather conditions, especially wind, before starting and while maintaining the blaze. To control a fire, they make firebreaks where they want the fire to stop. First, they burn a wide strip of trees, shrubs, or grass. Then, they wet the charred area. The fire roars toward this area. But when it reaches the firebreak, it runs out of fuel. It goes out.

# Wildfire!

Humans have an uneasy relationship with fire. Depending upon the situation, fire can be our friend or foe. As a friend, fire offers warmth, light, and heat for cooking. As a foe, an out-of-control fire can wreck property and bring death.

You may have seen Smokey the Bear on signs. He wears a hat and holds a shovel. His sign states, "Only YOU can prevent wildfires." Perhaps you've seen ads in which Smokey tells you not to burn trash and to be sure you put out campfires. Smokey was a real bear cub. He was rescued from a wildfire in New Mexico. He has been a fire prevention symbol for more than sixty-five years.

Wildfires are bad for humans and wild animals. Each year, these fires wreck millions of acres. They cost billions of dollars in property loss. Such blazes occur most often in hot, dry places. California, Texas, and Colorado are often hit. In years with little rainfall, dry tinder is everywhere. Nine out of every ten wildfires are started by a person, although rarely on purpose. A dropped cigarette, burning trash, or a child playing with matches can start a huge disaster.

Lightning strikes have started wildfires since Earth began. Left to burn, such a fire will clear out a stand of trees every eight to fifteen years. Fire is part of a natural cycle. Blazes allow forests to change. They free up the nutrients trapped in old, dead wood. Of course, many old-growth trees survive the flames because their bark can regrow.

Then, people created state and national parks and built homes near forests. When lightning started a blaze, people put it out. They did not want to lose their parklands, homes, or businesses to flames. For years, fires started by lightning were **suppressed**.

Then, in 1988, a huge fire destroyed part of Yellowstone National Park. People saw that fire suppression had backfired. Fire suppression had let fuel pile up for years. There were a lot of leaves, branches, and dead trees lying in the forests. Also, when fire does not clear an area, too many trees

grow. They get crowded and grow weak. There is a limited supply of water, sunlight, and nutrients. The trees fall victim to insects and diseases. Scientists realized that they had to find ways to allow fires to clear wooded areas without hurting people, property, or wild animals. The National Parks Department changed its fire-suppression policy.

Now, lightning-strike fires are allowed to burn if they will not affect the safety of people. Fire teams use controlled burns to start blazes in fire-dependent ecosystems. This reduces the fuel for wildfires. They must be careful not to let the fire get out of hand. They consider weather conditions, especially wind patterns, before starting and while maintaining the blaze. How do they control a fire? They create firebreaks where they want the blaze to stop. First, they burn a wide strip of trees, shrubs, or grass, and then they wet the charred area. The fire roars toward this area, but when it reaches the firebreak, it runs out of fuel and goes out.

# Wildfire!

Humans have long had an uneasy relationship with fire. Depending upon the situation, fire can be our friend or foe. As a friend, fire offers warmth, light, and heat for cooking. As a foe, an out-of-control fire can be destructive and deadly.

You may have seen Smokey the Bear on roadside signs. He wears a hat and holds a shovel. His sign states, "Only YOU can prevent wildfires." Perhaps you've seen ads in which Smokey tells you not to burn trash and to thoroughly extinguish any campfire. Smokey was a real bear cub rescued by firefighters from a wildfire in New Mexico. He has been the symbol of fire prevention for more than sixty-five years.

Wildfires are dangerous to humans and wild animals. Each year, such fires ruin millions of acres and cost billions of dollars in property loss. Such blazes occur often in places with hot, dry environments, such as California, Texas, and Colorado. In years with little rainfall, dry tinder is everywhere. Nine out of every ten wildfires are started by a person, although usually not on purpose. A carelessly dropped cigarette, burning trash, or someone playing with matches can start a disaster of immense proportions.

Lightning strikes have been starting wildfires since Earth began. Left to burn freely, such a fire will clear out a stand of trees every eight to fifteen years. Fire is part of a natural cycle. Blazes allow forests to rejuvenate because they release nutrients trapped in old, dead wood. Many old-growth trees survive the flames because their bark can regrow.

Then, when people created state and national parks and built homes near forests, wildfires started by lightning were **suppressed**. When lightning started a fire, people didn't let it burn. They fought back to protect parklands, homes, and businesses from the flames.

Then, in 1988, a massive fire decimated part of Yellowstone National Park. People realized that fire suppression had backfired. Fire suppression had allowed fuel to accumulate. There were a lot of fallen leaves, branches, and dead trees cluttering the forests. Also, when fire does not clear an area, overcrowding

results in weakened trees. They must compete for a limited supply of water, nutrients, and sunlight. Over time, trees become vulnerable to insects and diseases. Scientists realized that they had to find ways to allow fires to clear wooded areas without posing a hazard to people, property, or wild animals. The National Parks Department changed its fire-suppression policy.

Today, lightning-strike fires are left to burn in areas that will not affect people. Fire teams start controlled burns in fire-dependent ecosystems to safely reduce the amount of fuel for wildfires. The firefighters must be careful not to let the fire get out of hand. They consider weather conditions, especially wind patterns, before starting and while maintaining the blaze. To control a fire, they create firebreaks where they want the blaze to stop. How? They burn a wide strip of trees, shrubs, or grass. Then, they wet the charred area. The fire roars toward this area. But when it reaches the firebreak, it runs out of fuel and goes out.

# Wildfire!

**Directions: Darken the best answer choice.**

1. In the United States, most wildfires are started by
   Ⓐ fire teams.
   Ⓑ lightning.
   Ⓒ animals.
   Ⓓ careless people.

2. The word **suppressed** means
   Ⓐ stopped.
   Ⓑ encouraged.
   Ⓒ illegal.
   Ⓓ terrifying.

3. Which event happened last?
   Ⓐ The U.S. National Parks Department fought all fires.
   Ⓑ The U.S. National Parks Department changed its policy of total fire suppression.
   Ⓒ A bear cub named Smokey was rescued from a wildfire.
   Ⓓ A lightning strike caused a massive wildfire in Yellowstone National Park.

4. A firebreak is used to
   Ⓐ start a controlled fire.
   Ⓑ stop a controlled fire or a wildfire.
   Ⓒ burn a forest so new growth can occur.
   Ⓓ affect weather conditions.

5. A wildfire is more likely to happen in Texas than in
   Ⓐ California.
   Ⓑ Colorado.
   Ⓒ New Mexico.
   Ⓓ Washington, D.C.

6. A controlled burn is preferable to a lightning-strike fire because
   Ⓐ there will be no surprises or difficulties in fighting the fire.
   Ⓑ it takes more people to fight a controlled burn.
   Ⓒ it can be planned in advance.
   Ⓓ it can be left to burn itself out without any supervision.

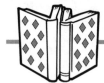

# A Major Disaster: The Indian Ocean Tsunami of 2004

The Indian Ocean Tsunami of 2004 killed nearly 300,000 people in Southeast Asia. It happened on December 26, 2004. A tsunami is made up of massive waves. They speed across the ocean and crash onto shore. It's hard to imagine the size of these waves. Some of them were as tall as an eleven-story building!

The giant waves came from a strong earthquake. It occurred on the floor of the Indian Ocean. It was stronger than all of the world's earthquakes since 1998 combined! Scientists think that it had the power of 23,000 atomic bombs. It made Earth wobble on its axis and spin slightly faster. The quake occurred at about 8:00 a.m. It was just 155 miles off the shore of Sumatra. It shook for four minutes. Those few minutes caused the worst tsunami of modern times.

Most tsunamis occur in the Pacific Ocean. They often come from undersea earthquakes. But that's not the only cause. Landslides that change the seafloor or volcanic eruptions on islands can also cause them. The seabed heaves up. This displaces a lot of water. That's what forms the waves of a tsunami. Ships at sea are not in danger. The water goes right under them.

Scientists know that warning people to flee is the only course of action once a tsunami forms. They have put sensors on the ocean floor that keep track of the depth of the water above. These sensors send data to a buoy. The buoy sends the information to a satellite. From there, it is beamed to the Pacific Tsunami Warning Center in Hawaii. Sadly, there were none of these sensors in the Indian Ocean. So the people in Sumatra and other parts of Indonesia had no warning.

Just fifteen minutes after the quake, the first giant wave reached northern Sumatra. It crashed onto the coast. It drowned everything in its path. Then, the water **receded**. It dragged the dead and the living out to sea. Rescuers rushed to the beach. They hoped to find survivors. Then, another huge wall of water appeared. It raced toward them at more than 500 miles an hour. No one could outrun it. Aftershocks caused more giant waves over the next seven hours. The waves did not follow a pattern. They damaged twelve nations.

Sumatra took the worst hit. Whole towns vanished. So did everyone in them. In some places, the waves reached more than one mile inland. Afterwards, people were buried in mass graves. There was not enough food and clean water. The whole region was declared a disaster area. It took years for the towns to be rebuilt. And many people were too scared to go back. They did not want to live near a coast again.

Now, a warning system has been put in the Indian Ocean. It is just like the one in the Pacific. It is there to keep a disaster like this from ever occurring again.

# A Major Disaster:
# The Indian Ocean Tsunami of 2004

The Indian Ocean Tsunami of 2004 killed nearly 300,000 people in Southeast Asia. It happened on December 26, 2004. A tsunami is a series of massive waves that crash onto shore. It's hard to imagine the size of these waves. Some of them were as tall as an eleven-story building!

The giant waves were the result of a strong earthquake. It occurred on the floor of the Indian Ocean. It was more powerful than all of the world's earthquakes since 1998 combined! Scientists believe that it had the power of 23,000 atomic bombs. It actually made Earth wobble on its axis and spin slightly faster. The quake occurred at about 8:00 a.m. It happened just 155 miles off the shore of Sumatra. It shook for four minutes. Those few minutes caused the worst tsunami of modern times.

Most tsunamis occur in the Pacific Ocean. They are usually the result of undersea earthquakes in shallow water. But that's not the only cause. Landslides that change the seafloor or volcanic eruptions on islands or near a shore can also cause them. As the seabed heaves upward, it displaces huge amounts of water. This forms the waves of a tsunami. Ships at sea are not in danger because the water goes right under them.

Scientists know that warning people to flee is the only course of action once a tsunami forms. They have put sensors on the ocean floor to monitor the depth of the water above. These sensors send data to a buoy. The buoy sends the information to a satellite. From there, it is beamed to the Pacific Tsunami Warning Center in Hawaii. Sadly, there were none of these sensors in the Indian Ocean. The people in Sumatra and other parts of Indonesia had no warning.

Just fifteen minutes after the quake, the first giant wave reached northern Sumatra. It crashed onto the coast, drowning everything in its path. Then, the water **receded**. It dragged the dead and the living out to sea. Rescuers rushed to the beach to look for survivors. While they were there, another huge wall of water appeared. It raced toward them at more than 500 miles an hour. No one could outrun it. Over the next seven hours, several more giant waves hit the shore. These waves, caused by aftershocks, did not follow any pattern. They battered twelve nations.

Sumatra suffered the worst hit. Whole villages and everyone in them vanished. In some places, the waves reached more than one mile inland. Afterwards, people were buried in mass graves. Food and clean water were in short supply. The whole region was declared a disaster area. It took years for the villages to be rebuilt. And many people were too afraid to return. They refused to live near a coast ever again.

Recently, a warning system was put in the Indian Ocean that is just like the one in the Pacific. It is there to keep a disaster like this from ever happening again.

# A Major Disaster:
# The Indian Ocean Tsunami of 2004

The Indian Ocean Tsunami of 2004 killed nearly 300,000 people in Southeast Asia on December 26, 2004. A tsunami is a series of massive waves that crash onto shore. It's hard to imagine the size of these waves: some of them were as tall as an eleven-story building!

The giant waves were the result of a strong earthquake that occurred on the floor of the Indian Ocean. It was more powerful than all of the world's earthquakes since 1998 combined! Scientists believe that it had the power of 23,000 atomic bombs. It actually made Earth wobble on its axis and spin slightly faster. The quake occurred at about 8:00 a.m., just 155 miles off the shore of Sumatra. It shook for four minutes. Those few minutes caused the worst tsunami of modern times.

Most tsunamis occur in the Pacific Ocean. They are usually the result of undersea earthquakes in shallow water, but that's not the only cause. Landslides that change the seafloor or volcanic eruptions on islands or near a shore can also cause them. As the seabed heaves upward, it displaces huge amounts of water. This forms the waves of a tsunami. Ships at sea are not in danger, however, since the water goes right under them.

Scientists know that warning people to flee is the only course of action once a tsunami forms. They have placed sensors on the ocean floor to monitor the depth of the water above. These sensors send data to a buoy, which transmits the information to a satellite. From there, it is beamed to the Pacific Tsunami Warning Center in Hawaii. Unfortunately, there were none of these sensors in the Indian Ocean. The people in Sumatra and other parts of Indonesia had no warning.

Just fifteen minutes after the quake, the first giant wave reached northern Sumatra. It crashed onto the coast, drowning everything in its path. Then, the water **receded**, dragging the dead and the living out to sea. Rescuers rushed to the beach to look for survivors. While they were there, another huge wall of water appeared. It raced toward them at more than 500 miles an hour. Nobody could outrun it. Over the next seven hours, several more giant waves hit the shore. They came from aftershocks and weren't predictable. In all, twelve nations were battered by these deadly walls of water.

Sumatra suffered the worst hit. In some places, the waves reached more than one mile inland. Whole villages and everyone in them vanished. Afterwards, people were buried in mass graves. Food and clean water were in short supply, and the whole region was declared a disaster area. It took years for the villages to be rebuilt, and many people were too afraid to return. They refused to live near a coast ever again.

Recently, a warning system was installed in the Indian Ocean that is similar to the one in the Pacific. Its purpose is to keep a tragedy like this from ever happening again.

# A Major Disaster:
# The Indian Ocean Tsunami of 2004

**Directions: Darken the best answer choice.**

1. A tsunami cannot be the result of a(n)
   - (A) volcanic eruption.
   - (B) tornado.
   - (C) earthquake.
   - (D) underwater landslide.

2. The word **receded** means
   - (A) formed a wall.
   - (B) flooded the shore.
   - (C) surged forward.
   - (D) drew back.

3. Which event happened first?
   - (A) An underwater earthquake off the coast of Sumatra caused a tsunami.
   - (B) A tsunami warning system was put in the Pacific Ocean.
   - (C) A tsunami warning system was put in the Indian Ocean.
   - (D) Nearly 300,000 Southeast Asians died.

4. The greatest risk of a tsunami forming is in the
   - (A) Atlantic Ocean.
   - (B) Arctic Ocean.
   - (C) Pacific Ocean.
   - (D) Southern Ocean.

5. A tsunami
   - (A) can be a series of giant waves over time.
   - (B) is always just one gigantic wave.
   - (C) is predictable.
   - (D) poses more danger to ships at sea than people on land.

6. As a result of the Asian Tsunami, the survivors suffered from
   - (A) a lack of shelter, food, and clean drinking water.
   - (B) a series of tornadoes.
   - (C) landslides.
   - (D) a massive hurricane.

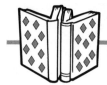

# Turning Waste into Fuel

Turning waste into fuel sounds great. After all, we must find a place to put the waste. And we'll always need fuel. How does this work? Biomass energy burns organic waste. Such waste includes plant stalks and sawdust. Burning creates heat. The heat boils water. The water turns to steam. The steam spins a turbine. This makes electric power. Another way to use waste is to trap and burn methane gas. This gas rises from landfills. It comes from **decomposing** trash.

Biomass is a renewable energy. We won't run out of it. Even so, it has problems. Burning biomass causes air pollution and greenhouse gases. It does make less of these than gas or oil. While it's stored before use, biomass can stink. No one wants to live nearby. Another issue comes up in hot weather. In the heat, plant biomass may burst into flames. It can do so without warning. This is called spontaneous combustion.

Scientists know how to run cars and buses on vegetable oil. It's called biofuel. It is a use for waste oil that has already been used. It was used to deep fry chicken or French fries. When biofuel burns, it smells like fried foods! But although it smells better than normal exhaust fumes, it still causes air pollution. It still makes greenhouse gases.

Pyrolysis may be the most promising use of biomass. This process superheats waste in the absence of oxygen. Plant matter is heated to 800°F. This changes it into gas and charcoal. Carbon dioxide is not produced with this method. It is the worst greenhouse gas. However, since pyrolysis needs high temperatures, it uses a lot of fuel.

Someday, turning waste into fuel may free the United States from needing foreign oil. Professor Thomas Seager hopes so. He is trying to make a device called a gasifyer. It will superheat any kind of waste and turn it into pollution-free fuel. He has a partner. Professor Fu Zhao has built a gasifyer. It is a stainless steel tube. It is eight feet long and about half a foot wide. The waste material and some water go inside. Then, they are superheated. In the end, the water will have toxins. They must find a way to clean the water. That will make the gasifyer more practical.

Their end goal is to make a movable machine that can accept any kind of waste. It will burn trash from a city. It will burn manure from a dairy farm. It will burn sawdust at a lumber mill. This machine will travel around and turn whatever waste is available into fuel. This would make it more economical than the biomass burners we have now. It would be more flexible, too. Today, each one can just handle one kind of waste, such as dried sewage. This practical, flexible, movable device may be decades away. Still, it is good to know that scientists are working on it. One day, it will be possible for us to turn waste into fuel.

# Turning Waste into Fuel

Turning waste into fuel sounds great. After all, we have to find a place to put the waste. And we'll always need fuel. How does this work? Biomass energy burns organic waste, such as plants or sawdust. The heat boils water. The water turns to steam. The steam spins a turbine. This makes electric power. Another way to use waste for fuel is to trap and burn the methane gas that rises from a landfill. This gas comes from **decomposing** trash.

Biomass is a renewable energy. We aren't going to run out of it. Even so, it has problems. Burning biomass causes air pollution and greenhouse gases. It does make less of these than gas or oil. Also, while it's being stored before use, biomass can stink. No one wants to live nearby. Another issue is that during hot weather, plant biomass may suddenly burst into flames. It can do so with or without warning. This is called spontaneous combustion.

Scientists have found ways to run cars and buses on vegetable oil. It's called biofuel. It is a use for waste oil that has already been used to deep fry French fries. When biofuel burns, it smells like fried chicken! But even though it smells better than normal exhaust fumes, it still causes air pollution and greenhouse gases.

Pyrolysis may be the most promising use of biomass. This process superheats waste in the absence of oxygen. Plant matter is heated to 800°F. This changes it into gas and charcoal. With this method, the greenhouse gas carbon dioxide is not produced. However, since it requires high temperatures, the process uses a lot of fuel.

Someday, turning waste into fuel may free the United States from needing foreign oil. Professor Thomas Seager hopes to make a device that can superheat any kind of waste and turn it into pollution-free fuel. He has a partner. Professor Fu Zhao has built a gasifyer. It is an eight-foot-long stainless steel tube. It is about half a foot wide. The waste material and some water are put inside. Then, they are superheated. Afterwards, the water will end up with toxins. They must find a way to clean the water. That will make the gasifyer more practical.

Once they've done that, their end goal is to make a movable machine that can accept any kind of waste. It will take trash from a city or manure from a dairy farm. This machine will travel around and turn whatever waste is available into fuel. This would make it more economical than the biomass burners we have now. It would be more flexible, too. Today, each one can only handle one type of waste, such as dried sewage. This practical, flexible, movable device may be decades away. Still, it is good to know that scientists are working to make it possible for us to turn waste into fuel.

# Turning Waste into Fuel

Turning waste into fuel sounds wonderful. After all, we have to find a place to put the waste, and we'll always need fuel. How does this work? Biomass energy burns organic waste, such as plants or sawdust. The heat boils water. The water turns to steam, which then spins a turbine. This makes electric power. Another way to use waste for fuel is to capture and burn the methane gas rising from a landfill. This gas comes from **decomposing** trash.

Biomass is a renewable energy source. We aren't going to run out of it. Even so, it has drawbacks. Burning biomass causes air pollution and greenhouse gases—although less than burning gas or oil. Also, while it's being stored before being burned, biomass can stink. Nobody wants to live nearby. Another hazard is that during hot weather, plant biomass may suddenly burst into flames without warning. This is called spontaneous combustion.

Scientists have found ways to fuel vehicles with vegetable oil. It's called biofuel. It is a use for waste oil that has already been used to deep fry onion rings and French fries. When biofuel burns, it smells like fried chicken! But even though it smells better than normal exhaust fumes, it still causes air pollution and greenhouse gases.

Pyrolysis is one of the most promising uses of biomass. This process superheats waste in the absence of oxygen. Plant matter gets heated to 800°F. This changes it into gas and charcoal. With this method, the greenhouse gas carbon dioxide is not produced. However, since it requires high temperatures, the process uses a lot of fuel.

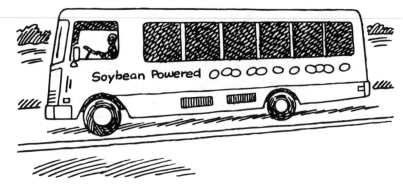

Someday, turning waste into fuel may free the United States from needing foreign oil. Professor Thomas Seager plans to create a device that can superheat any kind of waste and change it into pollution-free fuel. He is working closely with another professor, Fu Zhao, who has built a gasifyer. It is an eight-foot-long stainless steel tube that is about half a foot wide. The waste material and some water are put inside and superheated. Afterwards, the water will end up with toxins. They must find a way to clean the water to make the gasifyer practical.

Once they've done that, their end goal is to invent a movable machine that can accept any kind of waste—whether trash from a city or manure from a dairy farm. They want to invent something that can travel around and turn whatever waste is available into fuel. This would make it more flexible—and economical—than the biomass burners we have now. Today, each one can only handle one type of waste, such as dried sewage. This practical, flexible, movable device may be decades from becoming a reality. Still, it is good to know that there are scientists working to make it possible for us to turn waste into fuel.

# Turning Waste into Fuel

**Directions: Darken the best answer choice.**

1. The current problem with Seager's gasifyer is that
   (A) it takes too much energy to create the fuel.
   (B) the water ends up badly polluted by the process.
   (C) it creates a fuel high in carbon dioxide.
   (D) the device is enormous.

2. The word **decomposing** means
   (A) burning.
   (B) destroying.
   (C) rotting.
   (D) fresh.

3. Which event happens third?
   (A) Heat boils water.
   (B) Biomass energy burns plants.
   (C) Steam turns a turbine and creates electric power.
   (D) Water turns to steam.

4. Pyrolysis only works
   (A) with used vegetable oil.
   (B) when there is no oxygen.
   (C) at low temperatures.
   (D) when a gasifyer is present.

5. Spontaneous combustion has caused barns filled with straw to catch fire when
   (A) the straw suddenly burst into flames.
   (B) lightning struck the barn.
   (C) the straw suddenly turned into steam.
   (D) pyrolysis suddenly occurred.

6. A dead tree in the forest is an example of
   (A) pyrolysis.
   (B) gasifying.
   (C) methane.
   (D) biomass.

# Confucius and the Role of Government

"Governments are instituted among men, deriving their powers from the consent of the governed . . . Whenever any form of government becomes destructive . . . it is the right of the people to alter or to **abolish** it, and to institute a new government." Thomas Jefferson wrote these words. They are in the Declaration of Independence. They told the reason for the American Revolution. They were the guidelines by which our government was formed, too. Where did the ideas come from? Confucius. He was a man who lived 2,300 years before the American Revolution. He lived in what is now China.

**Confucius**

Confucius was a big, homely man. He was not rich. He was not powerful. But he loved learning. And he liked teaching. He had a group of followers. More joined him all the time. He lived during bad times. China was ruled by warlords. They just cared about getting richer. The system was awful. The nobles always had enough to eat. Yet the people who worked the fields often starved.

Confucius was born poor. His father died when he was little. As he grew up, he was thrilled by knowledge. He read every moment he could. He had a job. He got married and had two children. But his real love was learning. In his fifties, Confucius wandered around China. He met people in many provinces. He pulled together his thoughts. His wisdom was amazing. Many people were drawn to him. He welcomed anyone who wanted to be his student.

He is famous for his stand against corrupt government. What he said about people and their leaders has been repeated for more than 2,500 years. He said that any man could become a noble if he treated others fairly. He said that a king is only a king if he takes good care of his people. Government should be run by smart and honest men. People could overthrow any ruler who did not put their well-being first. He said that education would make all people equal. It would end classes in society. Learning should be for everyone, not just the rich. His ideas were new. They were shocking. Of course, the leaders of his time did not like him.

Confucius said that the truth must always be told. His followers kept spreading his ideas after his death. So Emperor Qin tried to kill them. He had the books of Confucius's sayings burned. But his students fled into the hills. Later, they overthrew the corrupt ruler. Over time, Confucius's teachings led to big changes. Government jobs were no longer given as favors. People were hired based on their scores on civil service exams. This let poor, yet smart, people be part of the government.

Confucius did not write down his thoughts. We know about them from the writings of his followers. They wrote down his conversations with them. The book is *Analects of Confucius*. His influence has lasted for twenty-five centuries. There is no sign of it fading away.

# Confucius and the Role of Government

"Governments are instituted among men, deriving their powers from the consent of the governed . . . Whenever any form of government becomes destructive . . . it is the right of the people to alter or to **abolish** it, and to institute a new government." Thomas Jefferson wrote these words. They are in the Declaration of Independence. They formed the basis of the American Revolution. They provided the guidelines by which our democratic government was created, too. Where did these ideas come from? They came from a man who lived 2,300 years earlier. His name was Confucius. He lived in what is now China.

**Confucius**

Confucius was a large, homely man. He was never rich. During his lifetime, he was not powerful. But he loved learning and teaching. He had a devoted group of followers. He got more and more over time. He lived during troubled times. China was ruled by warlords. They only cared about making themselves richer. The system was awful. The nobles always had enough to eat. Yet the common people who worked the fields often starved to death.

Confucius was born poor. His father died when he was little. His family had once been minor nobles. That was long before his birth. He was delighted by knowledge. He read every spare moment he could. He had a job, got married, and had two children. But his real love was learning. Eventually, Confucius wandered around China. He met people in the various provinces. He pulled together his thoughts. His wisdom was amazing. Many people were drawn to him. He welcomed anyone who wanted to be his student.

He is famous for his strong stand against corrupt government. What he said about people and their leaders has been repeated for more than 2,500 years. He said that any man could become a noble if he treated others with kindness. He said that a king is only a king if he takes good care of his people. Government should be run by talented and honest men. He said that people could overthrow any ruler who did not put the people's well-being first. He said that education would end classes in society. Education would make all people equal. Learning should be open to everyone, not just the wealthy. These ideas were shocking. Of course, he was not popular with the leaders of his time.

Confucius said that the truth must always be told. After his death, his followers kept spreading his ideas. Emperor Qin tried to kill them all. He ordered the books of Confucius's sayings to be burned. But his followers fled into the hills. They eventually overthrew the corrupt ruler. Over time, Confucius's teachings led to big reforms. Government jobs were no longer given as favors. They were awarded based on the scores on civil service exams. This let poor, yet smart, people be part of the government.

Confucius did not write anything down. We know about him from the writings of his followers. They compiled his conversations with them. They are all in the book *Analects of Confucius*. His influence has lasted for twenty-five centuries, and there is no sign of it fading away.

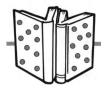

# Confucius and the Role of Government

"Governments are instituted among men, deriving their powers from the consent of the governed . . . Whenever any form of government becomes destructive . . . it is the right of the people to alter or to **abolish** it, and to institute a new government." Thomas Jefferson wrote these words in the Declaration of Independence. They explained the reason for the American Revolution. They also provided the foundation of the U.S. government. Where did these ideas come from? They came from Confucius, a man who had lived 2,300 years earlier. He lived in what is now China.

**Confucius**

Confucius was a large, homely man. He was never rich, and during his lifetime, he was not powerful. He loved learning and teaching and had a group of followers that grew bigger over time. He lived during troubled times when China was ruled by warlords who only cared about making themselves richer. The system was so corrupt that, while nobles always had enough to eat, the people who worked the fields frequently starved.

Confucius was born poor, and his father died soon afterward. His family had once been minor nobles, but that was long before his birth. He was interested in knowledge and read every spare moment he could. Although he had a job, was married, and had two children, his real love was learning. Eventually, Confucius wandered around China. He met people in the various provinces and formulated his thoughts. His wisdom was unparalleled, and many people were drawn to him. He welcomed anyone who wanted to be his follower.

He is famous for his strong stand against corrupt government. What he said about people and their leaders has been repeated for more than 2,500 years. He said that a man could become a noble if he treated others with compassion. He said that a king is only a king if he takes good care of his people. Government should be run by the brightest and most honest men. He said that people had the right to overthrow any ruler who did not put his people's well-being first. He said that education would eliminate classes in society and make everyone equal. Learning should be open to everyone, not just the wealthy. These ideas were revolutionary. His statements made him unpopular with the leaders of his time.

Confucius insisted that the truth be told. After his death, his followers kept talking about his ideas. Emperor Qin tried to kill them, and he burned all of the books of Confucius's sayings. But his followers fled into the hills and later overthrew the corrupt ruler. Over time, Confucius's teachings led to major reforms. Government positions were no longer granted as favors. They were earned by high scores on civil service exams. This allowed poor, yet smart, people to become a part of the government.

Confucius did not write down his teachings. We know about him from the writings of his followers. They compiled his conversations with them in a book. It is entitled *Analects of Confucius*. His influence has already lasted for twenty-five centuries, and there is no sign of it fading away.

# Confucius and the Role of Government

**Directions: Darken the best answer choice.**

1. How did Confucius affect the American government?
   - Ⓐ Some of his ideas are included in the Declaration of Independence.
   - Ⓑ He met with Thomas Jefferson to help him write the Declaration of Independence.
   - Ⓒ *Analects of Confucius* was the basis of the U.S. Constitution.
   - Ⓓ Both George Washington and Thomas Jefferson studied under Confucius.

2. The word **abolish** means
   - Ⓐ support.
   - Ⓑ create.
   - Ⓒ discuss.
   - Ⓓ eliminate.

3. Which happened third?
   - Ⓐ Confucius had many followers.
   - Ⓑ Confucius traveled around China.
   - Ⓒ The Chinese Emperor Qin ordered all copies of *Analects of Confucius* to be destroyed.
   - Ⓓ Confucius's followers overthrew Emperor Qin.

4. With which statement would Confucius agree?
   - Ⓐ Government leaders should always be women.
   - Ⓑ Government leaders must be concerned about their people's lives.
   - Ⓒ The government should only educate the children of the wealthy.
   - Ⓓ Only the rich should have children.

5. Confucius took a strong stand against people
   - Ⓐ rising up against an evil government.
   - Ⓑ reading a lot of books.
   - Ⓒ telling lies.
   - Ⓓ writing down his sayings.

6. What does *Analects of Confucius* prove?
   - Ⓐ Writing down a person's ideas allows them to have an influence on the world even after the person is dead.
   - Ⓑ A person can get rich from writing a book.
   - Ⓒ Writing ideas down is not a good way to preserve them.
   - Ⓓ Emperor Qin was a follower of Confucius.

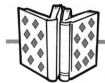

# Martin Luther and the Protestant Reformation

In 380 CE, the Roman Emperor Theodosius converted to Christianity. From then until the mid 1500s, the Roman Catholic Church dominated Europe. It was very powerful and didn't act much like a church of today. It commanded armies, fought wars, and decided the borders of nations. No one dared to question the Church's authority. No one, that is, until Martin Luther.

The Church and its leaders had become corrupt. They were more interested in becoming rich than telling the news about Jesus. Martin Luther was a monk in the Church. He was told to teach at a university in Wittenberg, Germany. He taught about the Bible. Lecturing on the Bible made him start to feel uneasy about the Church. For one thing, the Church had men going around selling indulgences. An indulgence was a piece of paper. It said that it would let a dead loved one's soul go to heaven. Some people sold all they owned. They bought one to be sure that their beloved dead went to heaven. Martin thought that this was shocking. It was **contrary** to what the Bible stated. So how could the Church get away with it? Only the Church leaders could read the Bible. It was written in Latin. People who did not know Latin could not read it.

On October 31, 1517, Martin nailed a paper to the door of the church at his college. It had ninety-five theses, or questions. He wanted the Church leaders to give proof from the Bible to support the things that were going on. Instead, the Church leader, the pope, was mad. He threatened to excommunicate Martin from the Church. This meant he would be thrown out of the Church. But Martin did not back down.

**Martin Luther**

The printing press had been invented. Martin wrote about the problems of the Church. He printed small booklets called tracts. People read them. They started to ask questions. The pope demanded that Martin come to the city of Worms. He wanted Martin to take back what he was writing. Martin went. But he would not take back what he had written. He said, "It is neither safe nor right to act against one's conscience. Here I stand; I can do no other. God help me." Then, the pope ordered that Martin be burned at the stake. It was a very painful way to die.

Martin had twenty days to live. Since he had been an important person in the Church, the pope still hoped that he would change his mind. Martin started for home. On the way there, his wagon was stopped by a group of men on horses. They kidnapped Martin. They took him to Wartburg Castle. The castle's owner, Prince Frederick, had grabbed the monk to save him. He kept Martin hidden in his castle for eleven months. During that time, Martin felt sad and lonely. Then, he decided to get busy. He made a translation of the Latin Bible. He wanted those who knew how to read German to read the Bible. This was the first time the Bible was translated for ordinary people to read.

Martin got to go home. The German princes protected him from the pope for the rest of his life. The protest that Martin started is the Protestant Reformation. Against his wishes, the people who followed him called themselves Lutherans. Today, the Lutheran Church is the third biggest Protestant group in America.

# Martin Luther and the Protestant Reformation

In 380 CE, the Roman Emperor Theodosius made Christianity the official religion of the Roman Empire. From then until the mid 1500s, the Roman Catholic Church dominated Europe. Unlike a church of today, it was a very powerful force, commanding armies, fighting wars, and determining the borders of nations. No one dared to question the Church's authority. No one, that is, until Martin Luther.

The Church and its leaders had become corrupt. They had lost sight of their mission. The Church was more interested in getting money than spreading the news about Jesus. Martin Luther was a monk in the Church. He was sent to teach at a German university in Wittenberg. He taught about the Bible. Lecturing on the Bible made him start to feel uneasy about the Church. For one thing, the Church had people going around selling indulgences. An indulgence was a piece of paper. It was supposed to let a dead loved one's soul enter heaven. Some people sold all they owned to buy one. They wanted to make sure that their beloved dead were safe in heaven. Martin thought that this was awful. It was **contrary** to everything the Bible stated. Yet the Church was getting away with it. Why? Only Church leaders could read the Bible. It was written in Latin. Ordinary people who did not know Latin could not read it.

On October 31, 1517, Martin nailed a paper to the door of the church at his college. It had ninety-five theses, or questions, that he wanted the Church leaders to answer. He asked for proof from the Bible to support the things that were going on. Instead, the Church leader, the pope, was enraged. He threatened to excommunicate, or throw out, Martin from the Church. But Martin would not back down.

**Martin Luther**

The printing press had been invented. Martin wrote about the problems of the Church. He had small booklets, called tracts, printed and handed out. People read them and started to ask questions. The pope demanded that Martin come to the city of Worms and declare that he was lying. Martin went, but he would not retract what he had written. He said, "It is neither safe nor right to act against one's conscience. Here I stand; I can do no other. God help me." Then, the pope ordered that he be burned at the stake.

Martin had twenty days to live. Since he had been an important member of the Church, the pope still hoped that he would say he was wrong. Martin started for home. On the way there, his wagon was overtaken by a group of men on horses. They kidnapped Martin and took him to Wartburg Castle. The owner of the castle, Prince Frederick, had grabbed the monk to save him. He kept Martin hidden inside the castle for eleven months. During that time, Martin felt sad and lonely. Then, he decided to stop wasting time. He made a translation of the Latin Bible. He wanted those who knew how to read German to be able to read the Bible. This was the first time the Bible was translated for ordinary people to read.

After Martin went home, the princes of Germany protected him for the rest of his life. The protest that Martin started is known as the Protestant Reformation. Against his wishes, the people who followed Martin called themselves Lutherans. Today, the Lutheran Church is the third largest Protestant denomination in America.

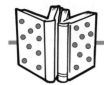

# Martin Luther and the Protestant Reformation

From 380 CE, when the Roman Emperor Theodosius converted to Christianity, until the mid 1500s, the Roman Catholic Church dominated Europe. Unlike a church of today, it was a very powerful entity, commanding armies, fighting wars, and determining the borders of nations. No one dared to question the Church's authority and power. No one, that is, until Martin Luther.

The Church and its leaders had become corrupt and lost sight of their mission. The Church was more interested in becoming wealthy than spreading the news about Jesus. Martin Luther was a monk in the Church assigned to teach at a university in Wittenberg, Germany. He taught about the Bible. Lecturing on the Bible made him start to feel uneasy about the Church. For one thing, the Church had people going around selling indulgences, papers that supposedly allowed a dead loved one's soul to enter into heaven. Some people sold all they owned to buy one and make sure that their beloved dead went to heaven. Martin thought that this was outrageous since it was **contrary** to everything the Bible stated. The Church was getting away with it because only Church leaders could read the Bible, which was written in Latin. Ordinary people who did not know Latin could not read it.

On October 31, 1517, Martin nailed a paper to the door of the church at his college. On it he had listed ninety-five theses, or questions, that he wanted the Church leaders to answer. He asked for Biblical proof to support the things that were going on. Instead, the pope, the Church's top leader, was enraged and threatened to excommunicate, or throw out, Martin from the Church. However, Martin would not back down.

The printing press had been invented. Martin wrote about the problems with the Church. His small booklets, or tracts, were printed and handed out to the community. People read them and started to ask questions. The pope demanded that Martin come to the city of Worms and declare that he was lying. Martin went, but he would not retract what he had written. Instead, he said, "It is neither safe nor right to act against one's conscience. Here I stand; I can do no other. God help me." Then, the pope ordered that he be burned at the stake.

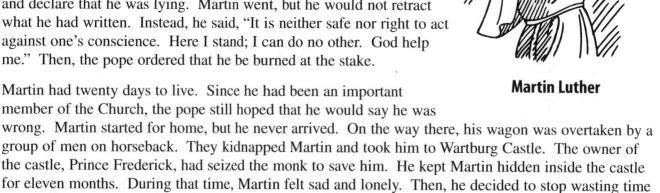

**Martin Luther**

Martin had twenty days to live. Since he had been an important member of the Church, the pope still hoped that he would say he was wrong. Martin started for home, but he never arrived. On the way there, his wagon was overtaken by a group of men on horseback. They kidnapped Martin and took him to Wartburg Castle. The owner of the castle, Prince Frederick, had seized the monk to save him. He kept Martin hidden inside the castle for eleven months. During that time, Martin felt sad and lonely. Then, he decided to stop wasting time and made a translation of the Latin Bible. He wanted those who knew how to read German to be able to read the Bible. This was the first time the Bible was translated for ordinary people to read.

After Martin returned home, the princes of Germany protected him for the rest of his life. The protest that Martin started is known as the Protestant Reformation. Against his wishes, the people who followed Martin called themselves Lutherans. Today, the Lutheran Church is the third largest Protestant denomination in America.

# Martin Luther and the Protestant Reformation

**Directions: Darken the best answer choice.**

1. Who saved Martin from a gruesome death?
   - Ⓐ the pope
   - Ⓑ the unnamed person who sent the ninety-five theses to Rome
   - Ⓒ Prince Frederick
   - Ⓓ the members of the Lutheran Church in America

2. The word **contrary** means
   - Ⓐ the same as.
   - Ⓑ the opposite of.
   - Ⓒ easily confused with.
   - Ⓓ certain.

3. Which event happened last?
   - Ⓐ Martin Luther was kidnapped by Prince Frederick.
   - Ⓑ Martin Luther posted his ninety-five theses.
   - Ⓒ Martin Luther was a teacher in the Roman Catholic Church.
   - Ⓓ The pope ordered Martin Luther to be burned at the stake.

4. Martin Luther wanted
   - Ⓐ to stay in Wartburg Castle for the rest of his life.
   - Ⓑ the Bible to be printed only in Latin.
   - Ⓒ the Roman Catholic Church to stop selling indulgences.
   - Ⓓ the people who followed him to call themselves Lutherans.

5. What first enabled Martin's ideas to spread around Europe?
   - Ⓐ Thousands of people visited him at Wartburg Castle.
   - Ⓑ Everyone in Europe could read his Bible translation.
   - Ⓒ Many people bought his indulgences.
   - Ⓓ His printed tracts were passed from person to person.

6. The Roman Catholic Church was the dominant, or main, force in Europe for about
   - Ⓐ 380 years.
   - Ⓑ 1,120 years.
   - Ⓒ 1,517 years.
   - Ⓓ 2,000 years.

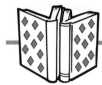

# The French and Indian War

The French and Indian War has an odd name. The war was not fought in France. It was not fought in India. And it was not a fight between the French and Indians! The war was fought in North America. It lasted from 1754–1763. It was a fight between the British and the French. Each nation wanted to own North America. The British and the French were already enemies. In Europe, they had been fighting each other on and off for hundreds of years.

British colonists wanted to move into the land west of the Appalachian Mountains. The French said that they could not settle there. France claimed it owned the whole area between the Mississippi River and the St. Lawrence River. It also said that it owned the five Great Lakes and the Ohio River Valley. To stop the British settlers from moving into this area, the French built some forts. The British began building forts as well.

Of course, all of this land was occupied by the Native Americans and should have belonged to them. But the French and British did not see it that way. The two nations fought bloody **skirmishes** for two years. Then, they declared war in 1756. Both European nations asked for help from the Native Americans who lived in the battle areas. Some Native American tribes sided with Great Britain. Other tribes sided with France. This meant that Native Americans fought on both sides of this war.

The Iroquois sided with the British. The Algonquin sided with the French. These tribes were already enemies. The war made things worse. Years later, these tribes saw that they should have stood together. They should have fought the colonists. They should have tried to keep their own land. Yet at the time, they did not think anyone could own land.

The French lost the war. At the Treaty of Paris in 1763, France gave up its claim to land east of the Mississippi River. It gave up Cuba, too. France still owned a lot of land west of the Mississippi. It gave some of this land to Spain. Spain was its ally. Then, Spain gave Florida to the British in trade for Cuba.

# The French and Indian War

The French and Indian War doesn't match its name. The war was not fought in France, and it was not fought in India. Nor was it a fight between the French and Indians! Instead, it was a fight between the British and the French. Each nation wanted to control North America. The British and the French had been enemies for centuries. In Europe, they had been fighting on and off for hundreds of years. They fought the French and Indian War in North America from 1754–1763.

France claimed it owned the entire area between the Mississippi River and the St. Lawrence River. In addition, it said it owned the five Great Lakes and the Ohio River Valley. British colonists wanted to move into the land west of the Appalachian Mountains. The French said that they could not settle there. To stop them, the French built some forts. The British began building forts as well.

Of course, all of this land was occupied by the Native Americans and should have belonged to them, but the French and British did not see it that way. The two nations fought bloody **skirmishes** for two years. Then, they declared war in 1756. Both nations needed soldiers. They asked the Native Americans living in the battle zones to help them. Some Native American tribes sided with Great Britain, and others sided with France. This meant that Native Americans fought on both sides.

The Iroquois sided with the British. The Algonquin sided with the French. These tribes had been enemies for a long time, and the war made things worse. Later, these tribes realized that they should have stood together to keep the colonists off their land. Instead, they helped fight a war that let other people take over their land. At that time, they did not think that anyone could own land.

The French lost the war. At the Treaty of Paris in 1763, France gave up its claim to all the land east of the Mississippi River. It also gave up Cuba to the British. France still owned a huge piece of land west of the Mississippi. It gave some of this land to Spain, its ally. Then, Spain gave Florida to the British in trade for Cuba.

# The French and Indian War

The French and Indian War has a name that just doesn't fit. The war was not fought in France, nor was it fought in India. It wasn't even a fight between the French and the Indians! The war was fought in North America from 1754–1763. The British and the French battled to see who would control North America. In Europe, these nations had been enemies for centuries, fighting each other on and off for hundreds of years.

British colonists wanted to move into the lands west of the Appalachian Mountains. The French wanted to stop them. The French claimed that they owned the whole area between the Mississippi River and the St. Lawrence River. The French said that they owned the five Great Lakes and the Ohio River Valley, too. Of course, all of the disputed land was occupied by the Native Americans. To stop the British settlers from coming into this area, the French built several forts. The British began building forts as well.

The nations fought many bloody **skirmishes** for two years before they officially declared war in 1756. Both European nations requested help from the Native Americans living in the battle areas. Some Native American tribes, including the Iroquois, sided with Great Britain. Other tribes, including the Algonquin, sided with France. That is how Native Americans ended up fighting on both sides of this war.

The Iroquois and Algonquin were already enemies, and this war made things worse. Many years later, they realized that they should have stood together. They should have fought both the French and British colonists. Instead, they helped to fight a war that gave other nations control of their land. However, at the time, they did not believe anyone could own land.

In 1763, France admitted defeat. At the Treaty of Paris, it gave the land east of the Mississippi River, plus Cuba, to the British. France still owned a huge tract of land west of the Mississippi. It gave some of this land to Spain, its ally. Then, Spain traded its colony in Florida to the British in exchange for Cuba.

# The French and Indian War

**Directions: Darken the best answer choice.**

1. The French and Indian War was a fight between the
   Ⓐ Algonquin and the French.
   Ⓑ Iroquois and the British.
   Ⓒ British and the French.
   Ⓓ French and the Native Americans.

2. The word **skirmishes** means
   Ⓐ legal arguments.
   Ⓑ terrorist attacks.
   Ⓒ disagreements.
   Ⓓ minor battles.

3. Which of these events happened last?
   Ⓐ The French tried to stop British settlers from moving west.
   Ⓑ The British owned Florida.
   Ⓒ The Algonquin and Iroquois chose sides.
   Ⓓ The British declared war on the French.

4. After the war, the French owned
   Ⓐ land east of the Mississippi River.
   Ⓑ land west of the Mississippi River.
   Ⓒ the island of Cuba.
   Ⓓ the Florida colony.

5. The Native Americans fighting in the French and Indian War did not realize that
   Ⓐ it would be better for them if the French won.
   Ⓑ it would be better for them if the British won.
   Ⓒ Spain was France's ally.
   Ⓓ no matter which nation won, the land would be taken away from them.

6. You are a British guard during the French and Indian War. You see a man slip into camp and go to confront him. The man will be safe if he is a(n)
   Ⓐ Iroquois brave.
   Ⓑ French soldier.
   Ⓒ Spanish soldier.
   Ⓓ Algonquin brave.

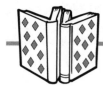

# The Lewis and Clark Expedition

Napoleon was the ruler of France. He owned a huge piece of land in North America. It was called the Louisiana Territory. He also had an island colony named Hispaniola in the Caribbean Sea. The western side of the island became the country of Haiti. The slaves in Haiti rebelled. Napoleon sent troops to stop them, but most of his men died from diseases. Then, a war with the British turned his attention closer to home. He lost interest in the New World. So he sold the Louisiana Territory to President Thomas Jefferson in April 1803.

Jefferson hoped there would be a waterway that went from the Mississippi River to the Pacific Ocean. No one knew since no one had explored the whole area. Jefferson hired Meriwether Lewis to explore and make a map of the new land. Lewis asked his friend William Clark to help him. In the winter of 1804, the pair hired forty-two men. They set up camp near St. Louis, Missouri. During the cold months, the men built boats. They practiced shooting. The trip's leaders bought gifts for Native American chiefs. They purchased beads, pipes, belts, and knives.

On May 14, 1804, the group set out in one fifty-five-foot keelboat and two smaller boats. Lewis and Clark thought that the round trip would take about eighteen months. Instead, it took them more than two years. During that time, the leaders kept logbooks. They drew pictures and made notes about plants and animals. Many were species that they had never seen before.

**Meriwether Lewis and William Clark**

Traveling by boat was hard. Rocks lurked below the surface of the water, ready to damage a boat that sailed into them. Where the water was too low, the boats had to be pulled or carried by the men. Thousands of mosquitoes attacked the men, and bears chased them. At last, they reached the Great Plains. There they shot and ate buffalo.

Then, the group met a Sioux tribe whose chief didn't like their gifts. He tried to **seize** one of their boats. In response, the men aimed their guns at the Sioux braves. The braves turned and left. After that, Lewis, Clark, and their weary group were glad to meet the friendly Mandan tribe. They spent the winter with them. In April 1805, they headed west again. They had three new members. A French trapper, his Native American wife, Sacagawea, and their baby boy came along. Sacagawea was helpful. She knew which plants they could eat and use as medicine. She saved their journals and other valuable things when a boat flipped. When the group needed horses in order to cross the Rocky Mountains, she got them from a tribe whose leader she knew.

Danger was a constant companion. One man was blind in one eye and had limited sight in the other. He accidentally shot Lewis! The group almost starved going across the Rocky Mountains. Yet just one man died on the trip, and it was from sickness.

The party returned home on September 23, 1806. The men had covered 7,700 miles in one of the biggest adventures of all time. The maps Clark made were only off by forty miles over the whole route!

# The Lewis and Clark Expedition

Napoleon, the ruler of France, owned the Louisiana Territory. It was a huge piece of land in North America. In the Caribbean Sea, he also owned an island colony named Hispaniola. The western side of the island became the country of Haiti. When the slaves in Haiti rebelled, Napoleon sent troops to stop them. However, most of his men died from diseases. Then, a war with the British turned his attention closer to home. He lost interest in the New World. So he sold the Louisiana Territory to President Thomas Jefferson in April 1803.

Jefferson hoped there would be a waterway that went from the Mississippi River to the Pacific Ocean. No one knew since no one had explored the whole area. Jefferson hired Meriwether Lewis to explore and make a map of the new land. Lewis asked his friend William Clark to help him. In the winter of 1804, the pair hired forty-two men and set up camp near St. Louis, Missouri. During the cold months, the men built boats and practiced shooting. The trip's leaders bought gifts for the Native American chiefs they might meet. They purchased beads, pipes, belts, and knives.

**Meriwether Lewis and William Clark**

On May 14, 1804, the group set out in one fifty-five-foot keelboat and two smaller boats. Lewis and Clark thought that the round trip would take about eighteen months. Instead, it took them more than two years. During that time, the leaders kept logbooks in which they drew pictures and made notes about plants and animals. Many were species that they had never seen before.

Traveling by boat was hard. Rocks lurked below the water's surface, ready to damage a boat that sailed into them. Where the water was too low, the boats had to be pulled or carried by the men. Thousands of mosquitoes attacked the men, and bears chased them. At last, they reached the Great Plains. There they shot and ate buffalo.

Then, the group met a Sioux tribe whose chief didn't like their gifts. He wanted to **seize** one of their boats. Fortunately, when the men aimed their guns at the braves, the Sioux left without putting up a fight. After that, Lewis, Clark, and their weary group were glad to meet the friendly Mandan tribe. They spent the winter with them. In April 1805, they headed west again with three new members. A French trapper, his Native American wife, Sacagawea, and their infant son joined them. Sacagawea was most helpful. She knew which plants they could eat and use as medicine. She saved their journals and other valuable things when a boat flipped. When the expedition needed horses in order to cross the Rocky Mountains, she got them from a tribe whose leader she knew.

Danger was a constant companion. One man, who was blind in one eye and had limited sight in the other, accidentally shot Lewis! The group almost starved going across the Rocky Mountains. Yet just one man died on the trip, and it was from sickness.

The party returned home on September 23, 1806. The men had covered 7,700 miles in one of the biggest adventures of all time. The maps Clark made were only off by forty miles over the whole route!

# The Lewis and Clark Expedition

Napoleon, the ruler of France, owned the Louisiana Territory, a huge piece of land in North America. In the Caribbean Sea, he also owned an island colony named Hispaniola, whose western side became the country of Haiti. When the slaves in Haiti rebelled, Napoleon sent troops to stop them. However, most of his men died from diseases. Then, a war with the British turned his attention closer to home, and he lost interest in the New World. So he sold the Louisiana Territory to President Thomas Jefferson in April 1803.

Jefferson hoped there would be a waterway that went from the Mississippi River to the Pacific Ocean. No one knew since no one had explored the entire region. Jefferson hired Meriwether Lewis to explore and create a map of the new land. Lewis asked his friend William Clark to help him. In the winter of 1804, the pair hired forty-two men and set up camp near St. Louis, Missouri. During the cold months, the men built boats and practiced shooting. The trip's leaders purchased beads, pipes, belts, and knives as gifts for the Native American chiefs they anticipated meeting along the way.

On May 14, 1804, the group set out in one fifty-five-foot keelboat and two smaller craft. Lewis and Clark thought that the round trip would take about eighteen months. Instead, it took them more than two years. During that time, the leaders kept journals in which they drew pictures and made notes about different plants and animals. Many were species that they had never seen before.

**Meriwether Lewis and William Clark**

Traveling by boat was difficult. Rocks lurked below the water's surface, ready to damage a boat that sailed into them. Where the water was too low, the boats had to be pulled or carried by the men. Thousands of mosquitoes attacked the men, and bears chased them. At last, they reached the Great Plains where they shot and ate buffalo.

Then, the group met a Sioux tribe whose chief disliked their gifts and tried to **seize** one of their boats. Fortunately, when the men aimed their guns at the braves, the Sioux left without putting up a fight. After that, Lewis, Clark, and their weary group were glad to meet the friendly Mandan tribe. They spent the winter with them. In April 1805, they headed west again with three new members. A French trapper, his Native American wife, Sacagawea, and their infant son came along. Sacagawea was helpful because she knew which plants they could eat and use as medicine. She saved their journals and other valuable things when a boat flipped. And, when the expedition needed horses in order to cross the Rocky Mountains, she got them from a tribe whose leader she knew.

Danger was a constant companion. One man, who was blind in one eye and had limited sight in the other, accidentally shot Lewis! The group almost starved going across the Rocky Mountains. Yet just one man died on the trip, and it was from sickness.

When the expedition returned home on September 23, 1806, the men had covered 7,700 miles in one of the biggest adventures of all time. The maps Clark made were only off by forty miles over the whole route!

# The Lewis and Clark Expedition

**Directions: Darken the best answer choice.**

1. When Napoleon sold the Louisiana Territory, the region became part of
   - (A) Hispaniola.
   - (B) Haiti.
   - (C) Canada.
   - (D) the United States.

2. The word **seize** means
   - (A) to take control.
   - (B) to fill with goods.
   - (C) to sink.
   - (D) to reject.

3. Which of these events happened second?
   - (A) Lewis and Clark set out with a team to explore the western part of North America.
   - (B) Lewis and Clark spent the winter with the Mandan tribe.
   - (C) Sacagawea joined the expedition.
   - (D) Lewis and Clark's men almost starved to death crossing the Rocky Mountains.

4. The primary goal of the Lewis and Clark expedition was to
   - (A) find and describe every new plant and animal species in the West.
   - (B) locate and trade with Native American tribes.
   - (C) find a water route to the Pacific Coast.
   - (D) learn Native American languages and discover their secrets to survival in the West.

5. Meriwether Lewis kept a logbook in which he wrote that Sacagawea helped to make their trip a success. Why?
   - (A) She brought along her infant son.
   - (B) She was married to a French trapper.
   - (C) She figured out what route they should take.
   - (D) She knew which plants they could safely eat.

6. Overall, the Lewis and Clark Expedition had
   - (A) good fortune because they gathered a lot of information and drew good maps.
   - (B) good fortune because they found a water route to the Pacific Coast.
   - (C) bad fortune because one of their boats flipped and everything was lost.
   - (D) bad fortune because so many of the expedition members died in the Rocky Mountains.

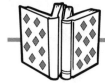

# The Spanish-American War

By 1500, the island of Cuba was under Spanish control. The Spanish treated the Cubans almost like slaves. In 1868, the Cuban freedom fighters rebelled. As a result, the Spanish governor had many people killed. The freedom fighters kept rebelling. But they did not succeed. In 1895, the Cubans decided to try a new method. They sent stories to American newspapers. They claimed the stories were true. But they were not. The papers' editors did not check the facts. They just printed the stories. Some were shocking lies. One article stated that the Spanish had killed one quarter of all Cubans. Then, they had eaten them!

Americans read these stories. They wanted to know why President Cleveland was not helping the Cubans. So in December 1896, Cleveland told the Spanish government to stop mistreating the Cubans. When McKinley took office in 1897, he agreed with Cleveland. He sent the ship *U.S.S. Maine* to Cuba. It was the first modern U.S. battleship. It took nine years to build. It was huge. It was longer than a football field. The ship arrived in Havana on January 25, 1898. Its captain got a note. It  was written in Spanish. It warned that the *Maine* would sink. The captain put the ship on alert. But it did no good. On February 15, the *Maine* blew up at 9:30 p.m. The ship's captain and most officers did not die. But 262 U.S. sailors were killed.

Some officers thought that the Spanish had hit the ship with a torpedo or a floating mine. Others said that the Cubans did it. Why? The Cubans may have wanted to start a war. They hoped America would win and **oust** the Spanish from Cuba. Two survivors said that they had heard a cannon blast. American experts studied the wreck. So did Spanish ones. The Americans said that the ship had touched a floating mine. The Spanish stated that one of the ship's boilers had blown up.

The real cause was unclear. Yet Americans were mad. On April 25, 1898, Congress declared war on Spain. The fighting lasted just 109 days. Spain gave up. It signed a peace treaty in December. It gave Cuba its freedom. America paid Spain $20 million for its colonies. They were Guam, Puerto Rico, and the Philippines.

But the questions about the *Maine* remain. Did the Spanish blow it up to make the Americans leave Cuba? Did Cuban rebels wreck the ship because they thought the Americans would get rid of the Spanish? Or did the ship's coal bunkers just overheat? Other ships built at that time had that trouble. If a bunker overheated, it could cause an explosion. Yet the *Maine* had an alarm. It was supposed to ring if the bunkers' temperature got too hot. It never sounded.

American William Randolph Hearst owned a newspaper. Newspapers sell best during wars. A photographer stated that Hearst sent him to Cuba to cover the war. But he did it before the ship blew up. When the man protested, Hearst is supposed to have told him, "You furnish* the pictures. I'll furnish the war." Did Hearst have a bomb planted on the ship? No one knows.

*Furnish: to provide or supply

# The Spanish-American War

By 1500, the island of Cuba had become a Spanish colony. The Spanish treated the Cubans a little better than slaves. So in 1868, the Cuban freedom fighters rebelled against them. In response, the Spanish governor had many people killed. The freedom fighters kept rebelling. But they had little success. In 1895, the Cubans tried a new tactic. They sent stories disguised as real news to American newspapers. The papers' editors did not check the facts. They just published the stories. Some were shocking lies. One article stated that the Spanish had killed one quarter of all Cubans and then eaten them!

Americans read these stories. They grumbled about how President Cleveland wasn't helping the Cubans. So in December 1896, Cleveland told the Spanish government to stop mistreating the Cubans. When McKinley took office in 1897, he agreed with Cleveland. He sent the *U.S.S. Maine* to Havana, Cuba. It was the first modern U.S. battleship. Longer than a football field, it took nearly nine years to build. The ship arrived on January 25, 1898. Its captain got a note written in Spanish. It warned that the *Maine* would sink. He put the ship on alert. Yet on February 15, the *Maine* blew up at 9:30 p.m. The ship's captain and most officers did not die. But 262 U.S. sailors were not as lucky.

Some officers thought that the Spanish had hit the ship with a torpedo or a floating mine. Others said that the Cubans did it. They wanted to start a war that they hoped would cause the Americans to **oust** the Spanish. Two survivors said that they had heard a cannon blast. Both American and Spanish experts studied the wreck. The Americans said that the ship had touched a floating mine. The Spanish said that one of the ship's boilers had blown up.

Although the real cause was unclear, Americans were angry. On April 25, 1898, Congress declared war on Spain. The fighting lasted just 109 days. Spain gave up. A peace treaty was signed in December. It gave Cuba its freedom. America paid Spain $20 million for its three colonies: Guam, Puerto Rico, and the Philippines.

But the questions about the *Maine* remain. Did the Spanish cause the explosion to make the Americans leave Cuba? Did Cuban rebels wreck the ship because they felt the Americans would get rid of the Spanish? Or did the ship's coal bunkers overheat? Other ships built at that time had that trouble. If a bunker overheated, it could cause an explosion. Yet the *Maine* had an alarm to let the sailors know if the bunkers' temperature was too warm. It never sounded.

American William Randolph Hearst owned a newspaper. Newspapers sell best during wars. A photographer stated that Hearst sent him to Cuba to cover the war before the ship blew up. When the man protested, Hearst purportedly told him, "You furnish* the pictures. I'll furnish the war." Could Hearst have had a bomb planted on the ship? Nobody knows for sure.

*Furnish: to provide or supply

# The Spanish-American War

By 1500, the island of Cuba had become a Spanish colony. The Spanish treated the Cubans practically like slaves. In 1868, the Cuban freedom fighters rebelled against the Spanish. The Spanish governor responded by killing many people. The freedom fighters kept rebelling, but without success. Then, in 1895, the Cubans tried a new tactic. They sent fictional stories disguised as news to American newspapers. The papers' editors did not check the facts. They just published the stories. Some were shocking lies: one article stated that the Spanish had killed and eaten one quarter of all Cubans!

When Americans read these articles, they wondered why President Cleveland wasn't helping the Cubans. So in December 1896, Cleveland told the Spanish government to stop mistreating the Cubans. When McKinley took office in 1897, he agreed with Cleveland. He sent the *U.S.S. Maine*, the first modern U.S. battleship, to Havana, Cuba. Longer than a football field, it had taken nearly nine years to build. Soon after the ship arrived on January 25, 1898, its captain got a note written in Spanish. It

warned that the *Maine* would sink. The captain put the ship on alert. Yet on February 15, the *Maine* blew up at 9:30 p.m. The captain and most officers survived, but 262 U.S. sailors were not as lucky.

Some officers suspected that the Spanish had hit the ship with a torpedo or a floating mine. Others said that the Cubans did it in order to start a war that would cause the Americans to **oust** the Spanish. Two survivors said that they had heard a cannon blast. Both American and Spanish experts studied the wreck. The Americans concluded that the ship had touched a floating mine. The Spanish insisted that one of the ship's boilers had blown up.

Although the real cause was unclear, Americans were angry. On April 25, 1898, Congress declared war on Spain. The fighting lasted just 109 days before Spain gave up. It signed a peace treaty in December that gave Cuba its freedom. America paid Spain $20 million for its three colonies: Guam, Puerto Rico, and the Philippines.

Even today, the questions about the *Maine* remain. Did the Spanish cause the explosion to make the Americans leave Cuba? Did Cuban rebels wreck the ship because they hoped that the Americans would get rid of the Spanish? Or did the ship's coal bunkers simply overheat? (Other ships built at that time had that trouble.) If a bunker overheated, it could cause an explosion. Yet the *Maine* had an alarm to warn if the bunkers' temperature got too hot, and it never sounded.

American William Randolph Hearst owned a newspaper. Newspapers sell best during wars. A photographer stated that Hearst sent him to Cuba to cover the war before the ship blew up. When the man protested, Hearst purportedly told him, "You furnish* the pictures. I'll furnish the war." Could Hearst have had a bomb planted on the ship? Nobody knows for certain.

*Furnish: to provide or supply

# The Spanish-American War

**Directions: Darken the best answer choice.**

1. The U.S. government paid money to Spain's government for
   Ⓐ the first modern battleship.
   Ⓑ the state of Maine.
   Ⓒ Cuba's freedom.
   Ⓓ three Spanish colonies.

2. The word **oust** means
   Ⓐ support.
   Ⓑ remove from control.
   Ⓒ disagree with.
   Ⓓ assist.

3. Which event happened third?
   Ⓐ William Randolph Hearst sent a photographer to Cuba.
   Ⓑ The *U.S.S. Maine* exploded and sank.
   Ⓒ President Cleveland told Spanish leaders to treat the Cubans better.
   Ⓓ The Cubans sent outrageous stories to the U.S. press.

4. Historians are certain that the
   Ⓐ Cubans blew up the *Maine* to get Americans to declare war on Spain.
   Ⓑ Spanish destroyed the *Maine* accidentally.
   Ⓒ destruction of the *Maine* brought about a war.
   Ⓓ Spanish set off a bomb on the *Maine* to get the Americans to leave Cuba.

5. Why might William Randolph Hearst have wanted to start this war?
   Ⓐ He could get rich selling war supplies.
   Ⓑ He was from Cuba and wanted the island freed from Spanish control.
   Ⓒ He wanted to rescue his photographer who was being held hostage by the Cubans.
   Ⓓ He wanted to get rich selling newspapers.

6. The Spanish-American War lasted less than
   Ⓐ one month.
   Ⓑ two months.
   Ⓒ three months.
   Ⓓ four months.

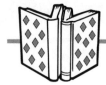
# Wilma Rudolph, Olympic Champion

Wilma Rudolph was the first American woman to win three gold medals during an Olympic Games. Yet when she was a child, that's the last **feat** anyone would have predicted for her. She was born in 1940. She was tiny and born too early. Still, she clung to life. Wilma was the twentieth child born to Ed and Blanche Rudolph. They would have two more children. They were poor African Americans. They barely made a living.

When Wilma had polio at the age of four, she was lucky to survive. It paralyzed her left leg. The doctor gave her a leg brace. He said she would never walk normally. Blanche ignored the doctor. She told Wilma that she would walk again. And she would do so with no leg brace and no limp! Blanche was an amazing mother. She would not give up. She found a college that had physical therapy. It was fifty miles away. She and Wilma made the one-hundred-mile round-trip bus ride twice each week. They did it for several years.

Wilma was amazing, too. Each day she had to do physical exercises that were painful and hard. But she never gave up. She kept on trying. At last, when she was twelve, she was able to walk without the leg brace. She was so thrilled that she took up running for fun. Soon it became clear that she was a gifted runner. At fourteen, she ran on her high school's track team. That's when a college track coach named Ed Temple saw her run. He put her on a special summer track team. It was for the best high school runners.

By the time she was sixteen, Ed had trained Wilma to the point where she became the youngest female on the U.S. women's track and field team. She was going to the 1956 Olympics! The Games would be held in Australia. It was a costly trip. Fortunately, some of the businessmen in her hometown of Clarksville, Tennessee, gave her the funds to go. She didn't disappoint them. Along with her teammates, Wilma won a bronze medal. It was for the 4 x 100-meter relay. Sports commentators said Wilma was "a force to be reckoned with." Everyone knew Wilma would be back for the 1960 Olympics.

Wilma's great running ability earned her a full scholarship to the University of Tennessee. This allowed her to take classes and run on the college's team. In 1960, she joined the U.S. women's Olympic team again. This time, the Games were held in Rome. Just a few days before her races, Wilma sprained her ankle! No one knew if she could run. It didn't look as if she would win any of the races. They need not have worried. Wilma won the gold medal in the 100-meter dash. Then, she won the gold in the 200-meter dash. To top it off, Wilma and her teammates won the 4 x 100-meter relay. Wilma made history on that day. Winning three gold Olympic medals is a major feat for anyone. It was incredible for a girl told she'd always need a leg brace.

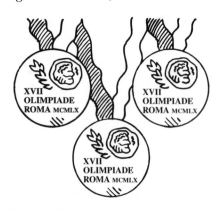

Wilma was called a hero. She was named Woman Athlete of the Year. In 1962, she retired from running. She worked as an elementary school teacher and running coach. In 1983, she was added to the U.S. Olympic Hall of Fame and, in 1994, the National Women's Hall of Fame. She died of a brain tumor on November 12, 1994. On that day, the world lost one of its most remarkable success stories. Wilma had proven that determination and hard work can bring about miracles.

Brief Biography

# Wilma Rudolph, Olympic Champion

Wilma Rudolph was the first American woman to win three gold medals during a single Olympic Games. Yet when she was a child, no one would have predicted she could do such a **feat**. She was born in 1940. She was small and premature. Still, she clung to life. Wilma was the twentieth of twenty-two children born to Ed and Blanche Rudolph. They were poor African Americans. They barely made a living.

When Wilma had polio at the age of four, she was lucky to survive. It paralyzed her left leg, and she had to wear a brace. The doctor said she would never walk normally. Blanche ignored him. She told Wilma that she would walk—and without a leg brace. She was an amazing mother who would not give up. She found a college that was fifty miles away. It offered physical therapy. She and Wilma made the one-hundred-mile round-trip bus ride twice each week for several years.

Wilma was amazing, too. Every day she had to do physical exercises that were painful and difficult. She never gave up and kept on trying. At last, when she was twelve, she was able to walk without the leg brace. She was so thrilled that she started running for fun. Soon it was apparent that she had a real talent for running. At fourteen, she ran on her high school's track team. That's when a college track coach named Ed Temple met her. He put her on a special summer track team for the best high school runners.

Ed trained Wilma. When she was sixteen, she became the youngest female on the U.S. women's track and field team. She was going to the 1956 Olympics in Australia! It was an expensive trip. Fortunately, some of the businessmen in her hometown of Clarksville, Tennessee, gave her the funds to go. She didn't disappoint them. Along with her teammates, Wilma won a bronze medal. It was for the 4 x 100-meter relay. Sports commentators called her "a force to be reckoned with." Everyone knew Wilma would be back for the 1960 Olympics.

Wilma's great running ability won her a full scholarship to the University of Tennessee. This allowed her to take classes and run on the college's team. In 1960, she qualified to join the U.S. women's Olympic team again. The Games were in Rome. Just a few days before her races, Wilma sprained her ankle! No one knew if she could even run, let alone win, any of the races in which she was enrolled. They need

not have worried. Wilma won the gold medal in the 100-meter dash. Then, she won the gold in the 200-meter dash. Finally, Wilma and her teammates won the 4 x 100-meter relay. Wilma made history on that day. Winning three gold medals in the Olympics is a major feat for anyone. It is astonishing for a girl who was told she'd always need a leg brace.

Wilma was hailed a hero and honored as Woman Athlete of the Year. In 1962, she retired from running. She became an elementary school teacher and running coach. In 1983, she was added to the U.S. Olympic Hall of Fame and, in 1994, the National Women's Hall of Fame. She died of a brain tumor on November 12, 1994. On that day, the world lost one of its most remarkable success stories. Wilma had proven that determination and hard work can bring about miracles.

# Wilma Rudolph, Olympic Champion

Wilma Rudolph was the first American woman to win three gold medals during a single Olympic Games. Yet when she was a child, that's the last **feat** anyone would have predicted for her. She was born, small and premature, in 1940. Still, she clung to life. Wilma was the twentieth of twenty-two children born to Ed and Blanche Rudolph. They were poor African Americans who barely made a living.

When Wilma was stricken with polio at the age of four, she was lucky to survive. It paralyzed her left leg, and she could only walk with a brace. The doctor said she'd never walk normally again. Ignoring what he said, Blanche told Wilma that she would walk again—and do it without a leg brace. She was an amazing mother who would not give up. She found a college that was fifty miles away that offered physical therapy. She and Wilma made the one-hundred-mile round-trip bus ride twice each week for several years.

Wilma was amazing, too. Every day she had to do a lot of physical exercises that were painful and difficult, but she never gave up. At last, when she was twelve, she finally was able to walk without the leg brace. She was so delighted that she took up running for fun. Soon it became apparent that she had a real talent for running. At fourteen, she ran on her high school's track team. That's when a college track coach named Ed Temple noticed her. He put her on a special summer track team for the best high school runners.

By the time she was sixteen, Ed had trained Wilma to the point where she became the youngest female on the U.S. women's track and field team. She was going to the 1956 Olympics in Australia! It was an expensive trip. Fortunately, some of the businessmen in her hometown of Clarksville, Tennessee, gave her the funds to go. She didn't disappoint them. Along with her teammates, Wilma won a bronze medal in the 4 x 100-meter relay. Sports commentators called Wilma "a force to be reckoned with." Everyone knew Wilma would be back for the 1960 Olympics.

Wilma's terrific running ability earned her a full scholarship to the University of Tennessee. This allowed her to take classes and run on the college's team. In 1960, she qualified for the U.S. women's Olympic team again. They went to Rome, but just a few days before her races, Wilma sprained her ankle! No one knew if she could even run, let alone win, any of the races in which she was enrolled. They need not have worried. Wilma won the gold medal in the 100-meter dash. Then, she won the gold in the 200-meter dash. Finally, Wilma and her teammates won the 4 x 100-meter relay. Wilma made history on that day. Winning three gold medals in the Olympics is a major feat for anyone, let alone a girl who was told she'd always need a leg brace.

Wilma was hailed a hero and honored as Woman Athlete of the Year. In 1962, she retired from running in order to work as an elementary school teacher and running coach. In 1983, she was added to the U.S. Olympic Hall of Fame and, in 1994, the National Women's Hall of Fame. She died of a brain tumor on November 12, 1994. On that day, the world lost one of its most remarkable success stories. Wilma had proven that determination and hard work can bring about miracles.

# Wilma Rudolph, Olympic Champion

**Directions: Darken the best answer choice.**

1. Wilma Rudolph won
   - (A) gold, silver, and bronze medals in the Olympics.
   - (B) gold and bronze medals in the Olympics.
   - (C) more Olympic gold medals than any woman in the world before or since.
   - (D) the first Olympic gold medal by a U.S. woman.

2. A **feat** is a(n)
   - (A) achievement.
   - (B) cash prize.
   - (C) academic honor.
   - (D) medal.

3. Which event happened third?
   - (A) Ed Temple trained Wilma to be a runner.
   - (B) Wilma competed in the Olympic Games in Rome.
   - (C) Wilma did painful exercises every day.
   - (D) Wilma competed in the Olympic Games in Australia.

4. When Wilma wowed the world with her Olympic success, she had already overcome
   - (A) being born with a paralyzed leg.
   - (B) having polio paralyze her leg.
   - (C) a brain tumor.
   - (D) a broken spine.

5. What worried Wilma's 1960 Olympic teammates?
   - (A) They knew she had just sprained her ankle a few days before the races.
   - (B) They didn't think she was good enough to be on the team.
   - (C) They feared her childhood handicap would hold her back.
   - (D) They didn't think the judges would let an African American woman win.

6. How many years passed between when Wilma first got the leg brace and Ed Temple discovered her talent?
   - (A) four
   - (B) eight
   - (C) ten
   - (D) twelve

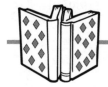

HOME
REAL GHOST STORIES
REAL GHOST PHOTOS
REAL GHOST AUDIO
TYPES OF HAUNTINGS
PARANORMAL INVESTIGATIONS

# Real Ghost Stories: Washington Irving

Washington Irving's ghost is one of the best documented in U.S. history. Many witnesses swore that they saw him. It seems fitting that the man who wrote *The Legend of Sleepy Hollow* should himself become a ghost. It is one of America's most widely read ghost stories.

Irving was born in New York City in 1783. He died there in 1859. In his lifetime, he was a lawyer and a writer. He was a businessman and a U.S. diplomat to England and Spain. He was the first American author to get international fame. European critics liked his writing.

Shortly after Irving died, Dr. J. G. Cogswell was working late. He was in Astor Library in New York City. Back then, a well-known, respected man could stay in the library after hours. Near midnight, Cogswell heard a noise. He went to see what made it. He had thought he was alone. Then, he saw a white-haired man. The man sat in a shadowy corner. The light was dim. Yet he was reading a book. Cogswell thought the man looked familiar. He moved closer. He was shocked to see that it was Irving. He had gone to his funeral just a month before! Irving was one of the founders of the library. He had spent many happy hours there. Three nights later, Cogswell saw the **specter** again. The ghost did not seem aware of the doctor. Yet each time Cogswell approached, it quickly faded away. For years to come, people saw Irving in the Astor Library.

Early in 1860, Irving's specter made another appearance. It was at his home in Tarrytown, New York. He walked through the house's parlor. He went into the library. That's where he had spent many hours writing. He did not go unnoticed. His nephew and two grandnieces saw him plainly. But when they rushed into the library, he was gone.

The man who made "the headless horseman" a household term and wrote *Rip Van Winkle* said that he did not believe in the supernatural. What must he have thought when he himself became a ghost?

Visitor number: 0032593                Last Site Update: 04/27/10

CONTACT US | REPORT A REAL GHOST STORY | NEXT WEB SITE IN THE RING

| HOME | |
| --- | --- |
| REAL GHOST STORIES | |
| REAL GHOST PHOTOS |  |
| REAL GHOST AUDIO | |
| TYPES OF HAUNTINGS | |
| PARANORMAL INVESTIGATIONS | |

# Real Ghost Stories: Washington Irving

Washington Irving's ghost is one of the best documented in American history. Multiple witnesses swore that they saw him. It seems fitting that the man who wrote *The Legend of Sleepy Hollow* should himself become a ghost. It is one of America's most widely read ghost stories.

Irving was born in New York City in 1783. He died there in 1859. In his lifetime, he was a lawyer, a writer, a businessman, and a U.S. diplomat to England and Spain. He was the first American author to gain international recognition. European critics enjoyed his writing.

About one month after Irving died, Dr. J. G. Cogswell was working late. He was in Astor Library in New York City. In those days, a well-respected man could stay after hours in the library to work. Near midnight, Cogswell heard a noise. He went to investigate. He thought he was alone. But he saw a white-haired man in a shadowy corner. Although the light was poor, the man was reading a book. Cogswell thought the man looked familiar. He moved closer. He was shocked to see that it was Irving. He had gone to his funeral just a month before! Irving was one of the founders of the library. He had spent many happy hours there. Three nights later, Cogswell saw the **specter** again. Although the ghost did not seem aware of the doctor's presence, each time Cogswell approached, it quickly faded away. For years to come, people would report seeing Irving in the Astor Library.

Early in 1860, Irving's specter made another appearance. It was at his home in Tarrytown, New York. He walked through the house's parlor and into the library. That's where he had spent many hours of his life writing. He did not go unnoticed. His nephew and two grandnieces saw him plainly. However, when they rushed into the library, he was gone.

The man who made "the headless horseman" a household term and wrote *Rip Van Winkle* said that he did not believe in the supernatural. What must he have thought when he himself became a ghost?

**Visitor number: 0032593**                    **Last Site Update: 04/27/10**

CONTACT US | REPORT A REAL GHOST STORY | NEXT WEB SITE IN THE RING

HOME
REAL GHOST STORIES
REAL GHOST PHOTOS
REAL GHOST AUDIO
TYPES OF HAUNTINGS
PARANORMAL INVESTIGATIONS

# Real Ghost Stories: Washington Irving

The story of Washington Irving's ghost is one of the best documented in American history. Multiple credible witnesses swore that they saw him. It seems fitting that the man who wrote *The Legend of Sleepy Hollow*, one of America's most widely read ghost stories, should himself become a ghost.

Irving was born in New York City in 1783. He died there in 1859. During his life, he was a lawyer, a writer, a businessman, and a U.S. diplomat to England and Spain. He was the first American author to gain international recognition. European critics applauded his writing.

About one month after Irving died, Dr. J. G. Cogswell was working late in Astor Library in New York City. In those days, a well-respected man could stay after hours to work in the library. Near midnight, Cogswell heard a noise and went to investigate. He had thought he was alone in the building. He saw a white-haired man sitting in a shadowy corner. The light was poor, yet he was intently reading. Cogswell thought the man looked familiar and moved closer. He was shocked to see Irving, whose funeral he had attended just a month before! Irving was one of the founders of the library. He had spent many happy hours there. Three nights later, Cogswell saw the **specter** again. Although the ghost seemed unaware of the doctor's presence, each time Cogswell approached, it quickly faded away. For years to come, many people would report seeing Irving in the Astor Library.

Early in 1860, Irving's specter made an appearance at his home in Tarrytown, New York. He strolled through the house's parlor and into the library. It's where he had spent many hours writing. He did not go unnoticed. His nephew and two grandnieces saw him plainly. Yet when they rushed into the library, he was not there.

The man who made "the headless horseman" a household term and wrote *Rip Van Winkle* often stated that he did not believe in the supernatural. What must he have thought when he himself became a ghost?

Visitor number: 0032593                    Last Site Update: 04/27/10

CONTACT US | REPORT A REAL GHOST STORY | NEXT WEB SITE IN THE RING

# Real Ghost Stories: Washington Irving

**Directions: Darken the best answer choice.**

1. Washington Irving wrote
   - (A) *Dr. J. G. Cogswell and The Headless Horseman.*
   - (B) *The Specter in Astor Library.*
   - (C) *Rip Van Winkle.*
   - (D) *Spanish Ghost Stories.*

2. The word **specter** means
   - (A) monster.
   - (B) ghost.
   - (C) author.
   - (D) soul.

3. Which event happened third?
   - (A) Dr. J. G. Cogswell said he saw Washington Irving's specter.
   - (B) Washington Irving wrote *The Legend of Sleepy Hollow.*
   - (C) The Real Ghost Stories Web site included the story of Washington Irving's specter.
   - (D) Washington Irving's relatives claimed his specter walked through his Tarrytown home.

4. What did Dr. Cogswell, Irving's nephew, and his two grandnieces have in common?
   - (A) All of them saw Washington Irving's ghost.
   - (B) All of them spent a lot of time in Astor Library.
   - (C) All of them lived in Tarrytown, New York.
   - (D) All of them lived in New York City.

5. From this passage, you can infer that Washington Irving
   - (A) enjoyed reading and writing.
   - (B) wanted to be a stage actor.
   - (C) wrote about the ghosts he saw at several different times in his life.
   - (D) did not enjoy his time as a U.S. diplomat.

6. The people most apt to visit the Real Ghost Stories Web site are those who
   - (A) do government research.
   - (B) think there is no such thing as a ghost.
   - (C) believe that supernatural events can happen.
   - (D) have never heard of Washington Irving's written works.

# New Zealand Daily Chronicle

## Pelorus Jack:  Famous Dolphin Feared Dead

**May 7, 1912**—It looks like our hero is dead.  His body has not been found.  Still, his twenty-eight-day absence indicates that he has **perished**.  For the past twenty-four years, Pelorus Jack has been on the job 365 days a year.  The only exception was a brief period of time.  It was while he recovered from an injury.  Those who will mourn his passing the most are the ship captains and crews.  They relied on him for their lives.

Pelorus Jack vanished just as mysteriously as he appeared.   In 1888, he popped up beside the *Brindle*'s bow.  It was at the mouth of the hazardous waters of the French Pass.  It lies near the New Zealand coast.  It was foggy and raining.  The crew thought that Jack, a Risso's dolphin, was a whale.  They wanted to harpoon him.  The captain's wife stopped them.   Instead, the *Brindle*'s captain followed Jack's path through the swift currents and sharp underwater rocks of the French Pass.  The ship reached its dock safely.

Wise seamen fear the French Pass.  It is a narrow strip of water that moves fast.  It has claimed dozens of ships and hundreds of lives.  But from that day on, Pelorus Jack escorted each ship that approached these hazardous waters.  First, he would frolic alongside a ship.  When it reached the French Pass, he would get in front of its bow.  He would stay there until the danger was past.  No ship that followed Pelorus Jack ever wrecked.

In 1903, a passenger on the *Penguin* shot Pelorus Jack.  The enraged crew turned on the man.  It took an order from the captain to keep the sailors from killing him.  Luckily, Pelorus Jack was just hurt.  He disappeared for two weeks.  During that time, he made a full recovery.  Then, he suddenly popped up out of the waters once more to guide ships.

He helped each ship that approached the French Pass, save one:  the *Penguin*.  How he recognized that ship is anyone's guess.  He never accompanied it again.  As a result, sailors quit the ship.  No one who knew its reputation would sign on for duty.  Not surprisingly, the *Penguin* wrecked in the French Pass.  Most of the crew and passengers drowned.

Immediately after he was shot, New Zealand passed a law.  It made it illegal to pester or hurt Pelorus Jack.   Since Risso's dolphins only live about thirty-five years, and he had been "on the job" for nearly a quarter of a century, Jack probably died of old age.  The number of ships, goods, and human lives he saved is beyond estimation.  We know it is extensive.   And so the staff of this newspaper wants to say:  Pelorus Jack, rest in peace.  You were a good and faithful pilot.  We wish that you had trained another like yourself.

# New Zealand Daily Chronicle

## Pelorus Jack:  Famous Dolphin Feared Dead

**May 7, 1912**—It looks like our hero is dead. His body has not been found, but his twenty-eight-day absence indicates that he has **perished**. For the past twenty-four years, Pelorus Jack has been on the job 365 days a year. The only exception was a brief period of time while he recovered from an injury. Those who will mourn his passing the most are the ship captains and crews who relied on him for their lives.

Pelorus Jack vanished just as mysteriously as he appeared.  In 1888, he popped up beside the *Brindle*'s bow.  This was at the mouth of the hazardous waters of the French Pass near the coast of New Zealand.  It was foggy and raining. The sailors thought that Jack, a Risso's dolphin, was a whale. They wanted to harpoon him, but the captain's wife stopped them. Instead, the *Brindle*'s captain followed Jack's course through the swift currents and sharp underwater rocks of the French Pass. The *Brindle* reached its destination safely.

Wise seamen fear the French Pass. It is a narrow strip of fast-flowing water that has claimed dozens of ships and hundreds of lives. But for twenty-four years, there was nothing to fear. From that day on, Pelorus Jack escorted each ship that approached the hazardous waters.  First, he would frolic alongside a ship.  When the vessel reached the French Pass, he would get in front of its bow. He would remain there until the danger was past. No ship that followed Pelorus Jack ever wrecked.

In 1903, a passenger on the *Penguin* shot Pelorus Jack.  The enraged crew turned on the man. It took an order from the captain to keep the sailors from killing him.  Luckily, Pelorus Jack was just hurt and disappeared for two weeks. During that time, he made a complete recovery. Then, Pelorus Jack suddenly popped up out of the waters once

more to guide ships.  He continued to help each ship that approached the French Pass, save one: the *Penguin*. How did he recognize that ship? No one knows. He never accompanied it again. As a result, sailors quit the ship, and no one who knew its reputation would sign on for duty. Not surprisingly, the *Penguin* wrecked in the French Pass, and most of the crew and passengers drowned.

Immediately after the dolphin was shot, New Zealand passed a law. It made it illegal to pester or hurt Pelorus Jack. Since Risso's dolphins only live about thirty-five years, and he had been "on the job" for nearly a quarter of a century, Jack probably died due to old age. The number of ships, goods, and human lives he saved is beyond estimation. We know it is extensive.  And so the staff of this newspaper wants to say:  Pelorus Jack, rest in peace. You were a good and faithful pilot. We wish that you had trained another like yourself.

# New Zealand Daily Chronicle

## Pelorus Jack:  Famous Dolphin Feared Dead

**May 7, 1912**—It appears that our hero is dead. Although his body has not been found, his twenty-eight-day absence indicates that he has **perished**. For the past twenty-four years, Pelorus Jack has been on the job 365 days a year. The only exception was a brief period of time while he recovered from an injury. No one will mourn his passing more than the ship captains and crews who relied on him for their very lives.

Pelorus Jack vanished just as mysteriously as he appeared. In 1888, he popped up beside the *Brindle*'s bow. This was in the treacherous waters of the French Pass near the coast of New Zealand. Due to fog and rain, the sailors thought this Risso's dolphin was a whale. They wanted to harpoon him. The captain's wife stopped them. Then, the *Brindle*'s captain followed Jack's course through the dangerous currents and sharp underwater rocks of the French Pass. The ship safely arrived at its destination.

All wise seamen fear the French Pass. It is a narrow strip of fast-flowing water that has claimed dozens of ships and hundreds of lives. But from that day on, Pelorus Jack escorted every ship that approached these hazardous waters. First, he would frolic alongside a ship until it reached the French Pass. Then, he would get in front of its bow. He would guide it through the danger zone. No ship that followed Pelorus Jack ever wrecked.

In 1903, a passenger on the *Penguin* shot Pelorus Jack. The enraged crew turned on the man. It took an order from the captain to keep the sailors from killing him. Fortunately, Pelorus Jack was only slightly hurt. After a two-week disappearance—during which he made a complete recovery—Pelorus Jack suddenly popped up out of the waters once more to guide ships.

He resumed helping every ship that approached the French Pass, except one: the *Penguin*. How he recognized that ship is anyone's guess, but he never accompanied it again. As a result, sailors quit the ship, and no one who knew its reputation would sign on for duty. Not surprisingly, the *Penguin* eventually wrecked in the French Pass. Most of the crew and passengers drowned.

Immediately after the dolphin was shot, New Zealand passed a law making it illegal to pester or hurt Pelorus Jack. Since Risso's dolphins only live about thirty-five years, and he had been "on the job" for nearly a quarter of a century, it is likely Jack succumbed to old age. The number of ships, goods, and human lives he saved is beyond estimation, but it is extensive. And so the staff of this newspaper wants to say: Pelorus Jack, rest in peace, you good and faithful pilot. We wish that you had trained another like yourself.

# Pelorus Jack:  Famous Dolphin Feared Dead

**Directions: Darken the best answer choice.**

1. The French Pass is a
   - (A) ship.
   - (B) sailing maneuver.
   - (C) kind of dolphin.
   - (D) waterway.

2. The word **perished** means
   - (A) died.
   - (B) disappeared.
   - (C) quit.
   - (D) retreated.

3. Which event happened third?
   - (A) Pelorus Jack helped the *Brindle*.
   - (B) A law made it illegal to pester, hurt, or kill Pelorus Jack.
   - (C) Pelorus Jack had a bad experience with the *Penguin.*
   - (D) The *Penguin* sank and most of the people on board died.

4. Why does the news reporter assume that Pelorus Jack is dead?
   - (A) He was shot, and no one's seen him since.
   - (B) Since he's been guiding ships for thirty-five years, he must be old.
   - (C) He's never been "off duty" for so long since he started guiding ships.
   - (D) He trained his offspring to guide ships, so he could die in peace.

5. The dolphin refused to guide the *Penguin* after 1903.  Why?
   - (A) The ship had struck and injured Pelorus Jack's mate.
   - (B) Pelorus Jack knew the ship was destined to be wrecked.
   - (C) Pelorus Jack knew that someone aboard that ship had shot him.
   - (D) Pelorus Jack knew the captain hunted and killed dolphins.

6. Reread the final paragraph of the passage.  You can tell that a pilot is a person who
   - (A) swims well.
   - (B) trains others.
   - (C) organizes cargo.
   - (D) guides along a path.

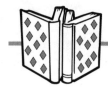

From:  justin@bigfamilies.com

Subject:  A Big Change

Date:  May 14, 2010

To:  favegrandma@bigfamilies.com

Hi, Grandma,

Today we went to the middle school to check it out. It's where I'll be going to school next year. I found out that there are things I'm going to like and dislike about going there. For one thing, it will be a big change. I've always been in the same elementary school. The middle school is much bigger. I'm a little worried about getting lost in the halls. Also, when classes passed, the halls were way too crowded. There were so many kids that it was almost impossible to move! Kids go to class without lining up as a group and then go to art or gym or wherever. I've always lined up and walked with the teacher and the rest of the group everywhere, so that'll be a big change for me. Plus, I didn't like how many people were in the hall. It seemed sort of **overwhelming**.

There were good things about the middle school, too. I like how you get to sit with your friends in the cafeteria. I've always had to sit with my class during lunch, so even if my best friend was in another class, I couldn't just go over and sit at his table. So that will be cool—that is, if we get the same lunch period. I also like the fact that I'll get a big locker all to myself instead of a coatroom. I like the fact that a locker is private, almost like having your own bedroom. I'll have to learn the combination, though, and they said you get detention if you get to class late. So I'll have to work my locker combination and make it through those clogged halls in just five minutes!

Next year they will change things so that there's a "school within a school." This means that one part of the school will be just for sixth graders. We'll pretty much stay in that part, although we'll still go to the library, cafeteria, and nurse's office with the other kids. I guess the school is so large that sixth graders have felt a little lost in the past. I can believe that! I'm glad they're making this change.

We went to some classes, too, and they were OK. The best part of the field trip was that we got to talk to some kids who are sixth graders. They were called "student ambassadors." They answered our questions in small groups. Then, they gave us their e-mail addresses, so if we think of more questions, we can ask them over the summer. I asked about fights. I don't want to get beat up by the eighth graders! My group's ambassador said that eighth graders pretty much ignore sixth graders, so they almost never pick a fight with one.

I'm going to be excited and scared to go to the middle school next year. I'm glad that Trisha has been there. She said that after one week, it will seem like home. I wish she was going to be in the middle school next year, too, but of course she's going on to high school.

Justin  :)

E-mail

From: justin@bigfamilies.com

Subject: A Big Change

Date: May 14, 2010

To: favegrandma@bigfamilies.com

Hi, Grandma,

Today we went to the middle school to check out where I'll be going to school next year. I found things I'm going to like and dislike about going there. For one thing, it will be a big change because I've always been in the same elementary school. The middle school is much bigger, and I'm a little worried about getting lost in the halls. Also, when classes passed, the halls were way too crowded. There were so many kids that it was almost impossible to move! Kids rush to class without lining up as a group and then go to art or gym or wherever. I've always lined up and walked with the teacher and the rest of the class everywhere, so that'll be a big change for me. Plus, I didn't like how many people were in the hall—it seemed sort of **overwhelming**.

There were good things about the middle school, too. I like how you get to sit with your friends in the cafeteria. I've always had to sit with my class during lunch, so if my best friend was in another class, I couldn't just go over and sit with him. Doing that will be cool—that is, if we get the same lunch period. I also like the fact that I'll get a big locker all to myself because a locker is private, almost like having your own bedroom. I'll have to learn the combination, though, and they said you get detention if you get to class late. So I'll have to work my locker combination and make it through those clogged halls in just five minutes!

Next year they will change things so that there's a "school within a school." This means that one part of the school will be just for sixth graders. We'll pretty much stay in that section, although we'll still go to the library, cafeteria, and nurse's office with the older kids. I guess the school is so large that sixth graders have felt a little lost in the past. I can believe that! I'm glad they're making this change.

We went to some classes, too, and they were OK. The best part of the field trip was that we got to talk to some kids who are sixth graders called "student ambassadors." They answered our questions in small groups and then gave us their e-mail addresses, so if we think of more questions, we can ask them this summer. I asked about fights. I don't want to get beat up by the eighth graders! My group's ambassador said that eighth graders pretty much ignore the fact that sixth graders exist, so they almost never pick a fight with one.

I'm going to be excited and scared to go to the middle school next year. I'm glad that Trisha went there first. She said that after one week, it will seem like home. I wish she was going to be in the middle school next year, too, but of course she's going on to high school.

Justin

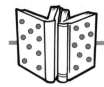

From: justin@bigfamilies.com

Subject: A Big Change

Date: May 14, 2010

To: favegrandma@bigfamilies.com

Hi, Grandma,

Today we went to the middle school to check out where I'll be going next year. I found things I'm going to like and dislike about going there. For one thing, it will be a big change because I've always gone to the same elementary school. The middle school is much bigger, and I'm worried about getting lost in the halls. Also, when classes passed, the halls were way too crowded. There were so many kids that it was almost impossible to move! Kids rush to class without lining up as a group and then go to art or gym or wherever. I've always lined up and walked with the teacher and the rest of the class everywhere, so that'll be different. Plus, I didn't like how many people were in the hall—it seemed **overwhelming**.

There were good things about the middle school, too, like how you get to sit with your friends in the cafeteria. I've always had to sit with my class during lunch, so if my best friend was in another class, I couldn't just go over and sit with him. Being able to do that will be cool—that is, if I have the same lunch period as my friends. I also like having a huge locker all to myself because a locker is private, almost like having your own bedroom. I'll have to learn the combination, though. They said you get detention if you get to class late, so I'll have to work my locker combination and make it through those clogged halls in under five minutes!

Next year the administrators will change things so that there's a "school within a school." One part of the school will only be for the sixth graders, and we'll pretty much stay in that section, although we'll still share the library, cafeteria, and nurse's office with the older kids. I guess the school is so large that sixth graders have felt a little lost in the past. I can believe that! I'm glad they're making this change.

We went to some classes, too, and they were OK. The best part of the field trip was that we talked to "student ambassadors" who are current sixth graders. They answered our questions in small groups and then gave us their e-mail addresses, so if we think of more questions, we can e-mail them this summer. I asked about fights because I'm afraid of getting beaten up by the eighth graders. My group's ambassador said that eighth graders pretty much ignore the fact that sixth graders exist, so they almost never pick a fight with one. That's a relief.

I'm going to be excited and scared to go to the middle school next year. I'm glad that Trisha went there first. She told me that after just one week, it will seem like home. I sure hope she's right! I wish she was going to be there next year, too, but of course she's going to high school.

Justin ☺

# A Big Change

**Directions: Darken the best answer choice.**

1. Justin is writing to tell his grandma about his
   - Ⓐ field trip to the middle school.
   - Ⓑ grades at the middle school.
   - Ⓒ first day at the middle school.
   - Ⓓ teachers in the middle school.

2. The word **overwhelming** means
   - Ⓐ way too little.
   - Ⓑ way too much.
   - Ⓒ fortunate.
   - Ⓓ unfortunate.

3. Which of these events has already occurred?
   - Ⓐ Justin has e-mailed his student ambassador.
   - Ⓑ The middle school administrators set up a school within a school for the sixth graders.
   - Ⓒ Trisha attended the middle school.
   - Ⓓ Justin attended the middle school.

4. Justin's student ambassador
   - Ⓐ made him afraid of the eighth graders.
   - Ⓑ told him the halls were too crowded.
   - Ⓒ gave out her phone number.
   - Ⓓ helped him to feel that the middle school would be a safe place.

5. You can tell that Trisha is probably Justin's
   - Ⓐ mother.
   - Ⓑ sister.
   - Ⓒ twin.
   - Ⓓ niece.

6. The "school within a school"
   - Ⓐ helps sixth graders feel that the building is a manageable size.
   - Ⓑ pairs each sixth-grade student with an eighth-grade student.
   - Ⓒ helps sixth graders learn their locker combinations quickly.
   - Ⓓ separates the students by academic ability levels.

# Man's Father and Son Shot On Same Date, Eighty-One Years Apart

Did you know that a famous U.S. president and his grandfather were shot on the same date more than eighty years apart? They had the same name and type of death. These are facts that few people know.

By the late 1700s, the Native Americans did not like white settlers. The newcomers were taking over their land. The Native Americans complained to the United States' leaders. But they were ignored. So the Native Americans went to the British in Canada. The British were eager to **undermine** the United States. The British had lost the Revolutionary War. They were still mad at the colonists. The British gave the Native Americans guns and bullets. They told them to kill the settlers.

In April 1784, Kentucky was the western frontier (edge) of the United States. A man named Abraham lived there. He had three sons. Each day, they all worked in the fields. One morning, they planted oats. That afternoon a shot rang out. The man fell to the ground. A Native American had shot him. Abraham died instantly.

The farmer's oldest son was Mordecai. He told the middle son, Josiah, to run to the fort. It was several miles away. Mordecai ran to the family's cabin. He got his father's gun. The youngest son was just six years old. His name was Thomas. He knelt beside his father's body and cried. The Native American who had fired the fatal shot crept out of the woods. He crossed the field. He seized Thomas. He raised his tomahawk. He meant to kill the boy. But just then, another shot rang out. Mordecai's bullet hit the Native American in the chest. It killed him. Mordecai saved his little brother's life. By doing so, he helped to set the course of American history.

Why? Thomas grew up. He had a son named Abraham. When Abraham grew up, he was the sixteenth U.S. president. Abraham Lincoln is one of the most important men in American history. He led the Union during the dark days of the U.S. Civil War. The Confederacy wanted to break away to form a new nation. Lincoln held the nation together. And he ended slavery. Yet he was the first U.S. president to be assassinated. This means he was killed while in office.

Eighty-one years after Thomas's father Abraham had been shot—on the same date—Thomas's son, Abraham, was shot! Just days after the Civil War ended, Lincoln went to see a play in Ford's Theatre. This was in Washington, D.C. The date was April 14, 1865. Just days before, Lincoln had had a bad dream. He dreamed that he would die. Unfortunately, it came true. Just after 10 p.m., a shot rang out. John Wilkes Booth, a well-known actor, had shot Lincoln. The bullet went into his brain. The president died early the next day.

It is common for a grandfather and his grandson to share the same name. But both of them being fatally shot on the same date eighty-one years apart is a fact stranger than fiction.

**Abraham Lincoln**

# Man's Father and Son Shot On Same Date, Eighty-One Years Apart

Did you know that a famous U.S. president and his grandfather were shot on the same date more than eight decades apart? They shared the same name and type of death. These are facts that few people know.

By the late 1700s, the Native Americans were upset with white settlers taking over their land. The Native Americans complained to the United States' leaders, but no one would help them. So the Native Americans went to the British in Canada. The British were eager to **undermine** the United States. They had lost the Revolutionary War and were still angry toward the colonists. The British gave the Native Americans guns and bullets. They told them to kill the settlers.

In April 1784, Kentucky was the western frontier (edge) of the United States. A man named Abraham lived there with his three sons. Each day, they all worked in the fields. They spent one morning planting oats. That afternoon a shot rang out, and the man fell to the ground. A bullet from a Native American's gun had killed him. Abraham died instantly.

The farmer's oldest son was named Mordecai. He told the middle son, Josiah, to run to the fort several miles away. Mordecai ran to the family's cabin. He grabbed his father's rifle. The youngest son, Thomas, was just six years old. He knelt beside his father's body and cried. The Native American who had fired the fatal shot crept out of the woods and crossed the field. He seized Thomas. Dragging him to his feet, he raised his tomahawk. He meant to kill the boy. But just then, another shot rang out. Mordecai's bullet hit the Native American in the chest and killed him. Mordecai had saved his little brother. Had he not, the course of American history would have been different. Why? Thomas grew up and had a son named Abraham. When Abraham grew up, he was the sixteenth U.S. president. Abraham Lincoln is one of the most important men in American history. He led the Union during the dark days of the U.S. Civil War. The Confederacy wanted to break away to form a new nation. Lincoln managed to keep the nation together. And he ended slavery. Yet he was the first U.S. president to be assassinated. This means he was killed while in office.

Eighty-one years after Thomas's father Abraham had been shot—on the same date—Thomas's son, Abraham, was shot! Just days after the Civil War ended, Lincoln went to see a play in Ford's Theatre in Washington, D.C. The date was April 14, 1865. Earlier in the month, Lincoln had had a nightmare that he would be killed. Unfortunately, it came true. Just after 10 p.m., a shot rang out. John Wilkes Booth, a well-known actor, shot Lincoln. The bullet went into his brain. The president died early the next morning.

A grandfather and his grandson sharing the same name is certainly not unusual. However, both of them being fatally shot on the same date eighty-one years apart is a fact stranger than fiction.

**Abraham Lincoln**

# Man's Father and Son Shot
# On Same Date, Eighty-One Years Apart

Did you know that a famous U.S. president and his grandfather were shot on the same date more than eight decades apart? They not only shared the same name, but they also shared the same kind of death. These are facts that few people know.

By the late 1700s, the Native Americans were angry because white settlers were taking over their land. The Native Americans protested to the United States' leaders, but their complaints were ignored. So the Native Americans went to the British in Canada. The British were eager to **undermine** the United States. They had lost the Revolutionary War and were still angry toward the colonists. The British gave the Native Americans guns and bullets and told them to kill the settlers.

In April 1784, Kentucky was the western frontier (edge) of the United States. A man named Abraham lived there with his three sons. Each day, they all worked in the fields. They spent one morning planting oats. That afternoon a shot rang out, and the farmer fell to the ground. A bullet from a Native American's gun had killed Abraham instantly.

The farmer's oldest son was named Mordecai. He told the middle son, Josiah, to run to the fort several miles away. Mordecai ran to the family's cabin and grabbed his father's rifle. The youngest son was six-year-old Thomas. He knelt beside his father's body, sobbing. The Native American who had fired the fatal shot crept out of the woods. He crossed the field and seized Thomas. Dragging him to his feet, he raised his tomahawk to kill the boy. But just then, another shot rang out. Mordecai's bullet hit the Native American's chest and killed him. Mordecai had saved his little brother and helped to set the course of American history.

When Thomas grew up, he had a son named Abraham. Abraham became the sixteenth U.S. president. Abraham Lincoln is one of the most important men in American history. He led the Union during the dark days of the U.S. Civil War. The Confederacy wanted to break away to form a new nation. Lincoln managed to keep the nation together, and he ended slavery. Yet he was the first U.S. president to be assassinated. This means he was killed while in office.

Eighty-one years after Thomas's father, Abraham, had been shot—on the same date—Thomas's son Abraham was also shot! Just days after the Civil War ended, Lincoln went to see a play in Ford's Theatre in Washington, D.C., on April 14, 1865. Earlier in the month, Lincoln had had a nightmare that he would be killed. Unfortunately, it came true. Just after 10 p.m., John Wilkes Booth, a well-known actor, shot Lincoln. The bullet lodged in his brain, and the president died early the next morning.

A grandfather and his grandson sharing the same name is certainly not unusual. However, both of them being fatally shot on the same date eighty-one years apart is truly a fact stranger than fiction.

**Abraham Lincoln**

# Man's Father and Son Shot
# on Same Date, Eighty-One Years Apart

**Directions: Darken the best answer choice.**

**1.** Abraham Lincoln has a large memorial in Washington, D.C., because he
  Ⓐ made sure the Native Americans' rights were protected.
  Ⓑ was the first U.S. president to be assassinated.
  Ⓒ enjoyed the theater.
  Ⓓ ended slavery in the United States.

**2.** The word **undermine** means
  Ⓐ support.
  Ⓑ start a war.
  Ⓒ ruin financially.
  Ⓓ work against.

**3.** Which event happened last?
  Ⓐ A settler named Abraham Lincoln was shot.
  Ⓑ Mordecai Lincoln shot a Native American.
  Ⓒ President Abraham Lincoln was shot.
  Ⓓ Thomas Lincoln had a son whom he named Abraham.

**4.** Josiah Lincoln was President Lincoln's
  Ⓐ father.
  Ⓑ uncle.
  Ⓒ brother.
  Ⓓ grandfather.

**5.** In 1784, Abraham Lincoln was shot on
  Ⓐ April 14.
  Ⓑ April 16.
  Ⓒ April 18.
  Ⓓ April 17.

**6.** John Wilkes Booth killed the president because the actor sided with the
  Ⓐ Confederacy.
  Ⓑ Union.
  Ⓒ Native Americans.
  Ⓓ British.

# Answer Sheet

**Name:** _____

**Title:** _____

**Page:** _____

1. Ⓐ   Ⓑ   Ⓒ   Ⓓ
2. Ⓐ   Ⓑ   Ⓒ   Ⓓ
3. Ⓐ   Ⓑ   Ⓒ   Ⓓ
4. Ⓐ   Ⓑ   Ⓒ   Ⓓ
5. Ⓐ   Ⓑ   Ⓒ   Ⓓ
6. Ⓐ   Ⓑ   Ⓒ   Ⓓ

# Answer Sheet

**Name:** _____

**Title:** _____

**Page:** _____

1. Ⓐ   Ⓑ   Ⓒ   Ⓓ
2. Ⓐ   Ⓑ   Ⓒ   Ⓓ
3. Ⓐ   Ⓑ   Ⓒ   Ⓓ
4. Ⓐ   Ⓑ   Ⓒ   Ⓓ
5. Ⓐ   Ⓑ   Ⓒ   Ⓓ
6. Ⓐ   Ⓑ   Ⓒ   Ⓓ

# Answer Sheet

**Name:** _____

**Title:** _____

**Page:** _____

1. Ⓐ   Ⓑ   Ⓒ   Ⓓ
2. Ⓐ   Ⓑ   Ⓒ   Ⓓ
3. Ⓐ   Ⓑ   Ⓒ   Ⓓ
4. Ⓐ   Ⓑ   Ⓒ   Ⓓ
5. Ⓐ   Ⓑ   Ⓒ   Ⓓ
6. Ⓐ   Ⓑ   Ⓒ   Ⓓ

# Answer Sheet

**Name:** _____

**Title:** _____

**Page:** _____

1. Ⓐ   Ⓑ   Ⓒ   Ⓓ
2. Ⓐ   Ⓑ   Ⓒ   Ⓓ
3. Ⓐ   Ⓑ   Ⓒ   Ⓓ
4. Ⓐ   Ⓑ   Ⓒ   Ⓓ
5. Ⓐ   Ⓑ   Ⓒ   Ⓓ
6. Ⓐ   Ⓑ   Ⓒ   Ⓓ

# Answer Sheet

Name: _____

**page 17**
1. Ⓐ Ⓑ Ⓒ Ⓓ
2. Ⓐ Ⓑ Ⓒ Ⓓ
3. Ⓐ Ⓑ Ⓒ Ⓓ
4. Ⓐ Ⓑ Ⓒ Ⓓ
5. Ⓐ Ⓑ Ⓒ Ⓓ
6. Ⓐ Ⓑ Ⓒ Ⓓ

**page 21**
1. Ⓐ Ⓑ Ⓒ Ⓓ
2. Ⓐ Ⓑ Ⓒ Ⓓ
3. Ⓐ Ⓑ Ⓒ Ⓓ
4. Ⓐ Ⓑ Ⓒ Ⓓ
5. Ⓐ Ⓑ Ⓒ Ⓓ
6. Ⓐ Ⓑ Ⓒ Ⓓ

**page 25**
1. Ⓐ Ⓑ Ⓒ Ⓓ
2. Ⓐ Ⓑ Ⓒ Ⓓ
3. Ⓐ Ⓑ Ⓒ Ⓓ
4. Ⓐ Ⓑ Ⓒ Ⓓ
5. Ⓐ Ⓑ Ⓒ Ⓓ
6. Ⓐ Ⓑ Ⓒ Ⓓ

**page 29**
1. Ⓐ Ⓑ Ⓒ Ⓓ
2. Ⓐ Ⓑ Ⓒ Ⓓ
3. Ⓐ Ⓑ Ⓒ Ⓓ
4. Ⓐ Ⓑ Ⓒ Ⓓ
5. Ⓐ Ⓑ Ⓒ Ⓓ
6. Ⓐ Ⓑ Ⓒ Ⓓ

**page 33**
1. Ⓐ Ⓑ Ⓒ Ⓓ
2. Ⓐ Ⓑ Ⓒ Ⓓ
3. Ⓐ Ⓑ Ⓒ Ⓓ
4. Ⓐ Ⓑ Ⓒ Ⓓ
5. Ⓐ Ⓑ Ⓒ Ⓓ
6. Ⓐ Ⓑ Ⓒ Ⓓ

**page 37**
1. Ⓐ Ⓑ Ⓒ Ⓓ
2. Ⓐ Ⓑ Ⓒ Ⓓ
3. Ⓐ Ⓑ Ⓒ Ⓓ
4. Ⓐ Ⓑ Ⓒ Ⓓ
5. Ⓐ Ⓑ Ⓒ Ⓓ
6. Ⓐ Ⓑ Ⓒ Ⓓ

**page 41**
1. Ⓐ Ⓑ Ⓒ Ⓓ
2. Ⓐ Ⓑ Ⓒ Ⓓ
3. Ⓐ Ⓑ Ⓒ Ⓓ
4. Ⓐ Ⓑ Ⓒ Ⓓ
5. Ⓐ Ⓑ Ⓒ Ⓓ
6. Ⓐ Ⓑ Ⓒ Ⓓ

**page 45**
1. Ⓐ Ⓑ Ⓒ Ⓓ
2. Ⓐ Ⓑ Ⓒ Ⓓ
3. Ⓐ Ⓑ Ⓒ Ⓓ
4. Ⓐ Ⓑ Ⓒ Ⓓ
5. Ⓐ Ⓑ Ⓒ Ⓓ
6. Ⓐ Ⓑ Ⓒ Ⓓ

**page 49**
1. Ⓐ Ⓑ Ⓒ Ⓓ
2. Ⓐ Ⓑ Ⓒ Ⓓ
3. Ⓐ Ⓑ Ⓒ Ⓓ
4. Ⓐ Ⓑ Ⓒ Ⓓ
5. Ⓐ Ⓑ Ⓒ Ⓓ
6. Ⓐ Ⓑ Ⓒ Ⓓ

**page 53**
1. Ⓐ Ⓑ Ⓒ Ⓓ
2. Ⓐ Ⓑ Ⓒ Ⓓ
3. Ⓐ Ⓑ Ⓒ Ⓓ
4. Ⓐ Ⓑ Ⓒ Ⓓ
5. Ⓐ Ⓑ Ⓒ Ⓓ
6. Ⓐ Ⓑ Ⓒ Ⓓ

**page 57**
1. Ⓐ Ⓑ Ⓒ Ⓓ
2. Ⓐ Ⓑ Ⓒ Ⓓ
3. Ⓐ Ⓑ Ⓒ Ⓓ
4. Ⓐ Ⓑ Ⓒ Ⓓ
5. Ⓐ Ⓑ Ⓒ Ⓓ
6. Ⓐ Ⓑ Ⓒ Ⓓ

**page 61**
1. Ⓐ Ⓑ Ⓒ Ⓓ
2. Ⓐ Ⓑ Ⓒ Ⓓ
3. Ⓐ Ⓑ Ⓒ Ⓓ
4. Ⓐ Ⓑ Ⓒ Ⓓ
5. Ⓐ Ⓑ Ⓒ Ⓓ
6. Ⓐ Ⓑ Ⓒ Ⓓ

**page 65**
1. Ⓐ Ⓑ Ⓒ Ⓓ
2. Ⓐ Ⓑ Ⓒ Ⓓ
3. Ⓐ Ⓑ Ⓒ Ⓓ
4. Ⓐ Ⓑ Ⓒ Ⓓ
5. Ⓐ Ⓑ Ⓒ Ⓓ
6. Ⓐ Ⓑ Ⓒ Ⓓ

**page 69**
1. Ⓐ Ⓑ Ⓒ Ⓓ
2. Ⓐ Ⓑ Ⓒ Ⓓ
3. Ⓐ Ⓑ Ⓒ Ⓓ
4. Ⓐ Ⓑ Ⓒ Ⓓ
5. Ⓐ Ⓑ Ⓒ Ⓓ
6. Ⓐ Ⓑ Ⓒ Ⓓ

**page 73**
1. Ⓐ Ⓑ Ⓒ Ⓓ
2. Ⓐ Ⓑ Ⓒ Ⓓ
3. Ⓐ Ⓑ Ⓒ Ⓓ
4. Ⓐ Ⓑ Ⓒ Ⓓ
5. Ⓐ Ⓑ Ⓒ Ⓓ
6. Ⓐ Ⓑ Ⓒ Ⓓ

**page 77**
1. Ⓐ Ⓑ Ⓒ Ⓓ
2. Ⓐ Ⓑ Ⓒ Ⓓ
3. Ⓐ Ⓑ Ⓒ Ⓓ
4. Ⓐ Ⓑ Ⓒ Ⓓ
5. Ⓐ Ⓑ Ⓒ Ⓓ
6. Ⓐ Ⓑ Ⓒ Ⓓ

**page 81**
1. Ⓐ Ⓑ Ⓒ Ⓓ
2. Ⓐ Ⓑ Ⓒ Ⓓ
3. Ⓐ Ⓑ Ⓒ Ⓓ
4. Ⓐ Ⓑ Ⓒ Ⓓ
5. Ⓐ Ⓑ Ⓒ Ⓓ
6. Ⓐ Ⓑ Ⓒ Ⓓ

**page 85**
1. Ⓐ Ⓑ Ⓒ Ⓓ
2. Ⓐ Ⓑ Ⓒ Ⓓ
3. Ⓐ Ⓑ Ⓒ Ⓓ
4. Ⓐ Ⓑ Ⓒ Ⓓ
5. Ⓐ Ⓑ Ⓒ Ⓓ
6. Ⓐ Ⓑ Ⓒ Ⓓ

**page 89**
1. Ⓐ Ⓑ Ⓒ Ⓓ
2. Ⓐ Ⓑ Ⓒ Ⓓ
3. Ⓐ Ⓑ Ⓒ Ⓓ
4. Ⓐ Ⓑ Ⓒ Ⓓ
5. Ⓐ Ⓑ Ⓒ Ⓓ
6. Ⓐ Ⓑ Ⓒ Ⓓ

**page 93**
1. Ⓐ Ⓑ Ⓒ Ⓓ
2. Ⓐ Ⓑ Ⓒ Ⓓ
3. Ⓐ Ⓑ Ⓒ Ⓓ
4. Ⓐ Ⓑ Ⓒ Ⓓ
5. Ⓐ Ⓑ Ⓒ Ⓓ
6. Ⓐ Ⓑ Ⓒ Ⓓ

# Answer Key

**page 17**
1. B
2. A
3. B
4. D
5. C
6. D

**page 21**
1. A
2. B
3. C
4. D
5. A
6. B

**page 25**
1. B
2. A
3. A
4. C
5. C
6. A

**page 29**
1. D
2. C
3. B
4. A
5. D
6. B

**page 33**
1. C
2. D
3. D
4. A
5. B
6. A

**page 37**
1. B
2. D
3. C
4. C
5. B
6. B

**page 41**
1. D
2. C
3. D
4. A
5. B
6. A

**page 45**
1. D
2. A
3. B
4. B
5. D
6. C

**page 49**
1. B
2. D
3. B
4. C
5. A
6. A

**page 53**
1. B
2. C
3. D
4. B
5. A
6. D

**page 57**
1. A
2. D
3. C
4. B
5. C
6. A

**page 61**
1. C
2. B
3. A
4. C
5. D
6. B

**page 65**
1. C
2. D
3. B
4. B
5. D
6. A

**page 69**
1. D
2. A
3. B
4. C
5. D
6. A

**page 73**
1. D
2. B
3. A
4. C
5. D
6. D

**page 77**
1. B
2. A
3. D
4. B
5. A
6. C

**page 81**
1. C
2. B
3. D
4. A
5. A
6. C

**page 85**
1. D
2. A
3. B
4. C
5. C
6. D

**page 89**
1. A
2. B
3. C
4. D
5. B
6. A

**page 93**
1. D
2. D
3. C
4. B
5. A
6. A